# THE SOFT FURNISHING BOOK

by
**Dorothy Gates** FAMU

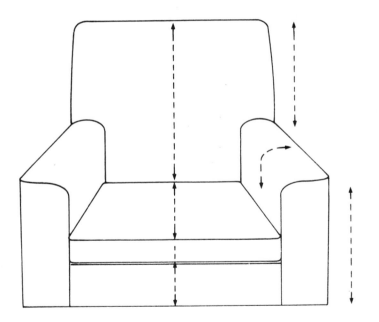

**fp**

F O R B E S   P U B L I C A T I O N S

*To my dear husband John and our sons Matthew and Jonathan*

*Chair featured on the front cover was
loaned by Gatestone Upholstery and
covered in calico. Loose cover was cut
by the author in Alessandra
ZH 446/2 from the Sanderson
linen union range.*

*Photographs by John Gates*

© Dorothy Gates

FORBES PUBLICATIONS LIMITED
Hartree House, Queensway,
London W2 4SH

Reproduced from copy supplied
printed and bound in Great Britain
by Billing and Sons Limited and Kemp Hall Bindery
Guildford, London, Oxford, Worcester

# Contents

# Preface

Craftsmen and women rarely have the time, or the inclination, to write about their craft. So unless they are able to teach an apprentice, their valuable knowledge is not passed on and is lost forever.

I have tried therefore, to write down all the processes in a simple manner, so that the reader may understand and follow the basic skill and craft of soft furnishing.

This book is intended to be a useful guide to the apprentice or student, and as a reference book for use on City and Guilds examination courses.

In the many aspects of Adult Education, this book should be useful as a guide or back up to demonstration.

However, it is not enough to read about a skill or craft. Practice makes perfect.

Dorothy A. Gates FAMU

# Introduction

Making new items for your home—or refurbishing older ones—is an extremely satisfying occupation for several reasons. Economically it makes sense—it is obviously cheaper to make your own soft furnishings than to pay someone else to do them for you. It gives you the choice to have exactly what you want, and the feeling of achievement when you can see your finished work enhancing your home is worth much more than money. Making a loose cover for an old settee gives great pleasure and the delight of feeling you have given a new lease of life to something that is basically well made, but was just a little shabby on the surface.

We hope this book will help you to produce perfect soft furnishings. The author is an expert on the subject and she passes on to you in a clear and factual way all the knowledge she has gained over the years. So, whether you are going to make new curtains, a loose cover for a much-loved chair or a duvet cover, may we wish you every success in your future soft-furnishing projects.

# Tools and equipment

The following list gives a guide to the basic tools and equipment needed:

Large oblong table
Sewing machine (one with a swing needle is an advantage)
Running foot
Piping foot
Machine needles (from 11 to 16)
Scissors (with at least 15cm blade)
Steel pins (3cm and 2½cm)
Metre stick
Tape measure
Assorted sewing needles
Iron
Ironing table
Notebook
Pencil

In addition the following items will prove very useful:

An assortment of coloured threads, both tacking cotton and sewing thread
Tailors' chalk
Small pair of scissors
Set square
Thimble
Heavy weight (used as an anchor for holding curtains in place when lining-in). This weight can be made from a house brick covered with fabric, it is among the most versatile pieces of equipment in use.
Extra spools for the machine to save time and thread wastage

# 1: Types of fabric and their uses

Choosing the right fabric for the job is essential. There is no point in spending time, money and effort making a loose cover for a much-used chair out of curtain fabric that will not wear for more than a year. The correct fabric will look better and last far, far longer. There is a multitude of fabrics to cover all soft furnishing needs—each with their own special uses and advantages.

When choosing a fabric to be made into curtains, covers, etc., ask yourself these questions: a) is it suitable for the purpose? b) will it clean or wash well? c) does it complement the existing furnishings?

When choosing from a pattern book, you will find that the manufacturer will state on the front cover the type of fabric, the most suitable use for it and how it should be cleaned.

When buying from a roll, look for the ticket in the centre; this will tell you the content of the fabric, e.g. 40% cotton 60% linen. Always ask for advice if you are not sure.

The following names of fabrics describe their type of weave or texture; they can be made from natural or man-made fibres, and can look almost identical. Many fabrics are now made of a mixture of fibres, just to add to the confusion.

## Fabrics to choose for curtains

*Brocade*   A fine woven fabric, looks embroidered, the back is striped. Usually the design is traditional. Made in silk, cotton, rayon or a mixture of man-made fibres.

*Bump*   A loosely woven fluffy fabric, used for interlining curtains. Made from cotton or synthetic fibres.

*Chintz*   A fine woven cotton, with a heavily glazed surface, available in plain colours but generally printed. Rather a stiff texture, it loses the glaze after several cleanings. Resists dirt.

*Calico*   Made in several qualities, usually unbleached. Needs to be pre-shrunk if used

for curtains. Popular at the moment when trimmed with braid. Cotton.

*Cotton*   Printed or plain, the texture is smooth with a close weave, it is hard wearing and looks crisp and fresh. Great variety of patterns available. Tends to shrink, so allowance must be made for this.

*Damask*   A self-patterned fabric, the weave is reversed on the back giving a light and shade effect. Made in silk, cotton, rayon, terylene.

*Dupion*   A plain coloured slub* fabric, with a silky look and a slub running across it. It has a satin back which can be in a different shade; this gives a shot silk effect. Fairly light, it drapes very well. Made in silk, rayon or a mixture of man-made fibres.

*Folk weave*   A tweed type fabric, rather heavy looking, but can be made in lightweight fibres. Many patterns in stripes, checks and plains available. Made from cotton, or man-made fibres.

*Gingham*   A fine cotton, woven in a check design, suitable for unlined curtains as it is reversible.

*Linen*   Can be smooth or coarsely woven, printed or plain.

*Linen union*   Mixture of linen with viscose or cotton. Sometimes mixed with a percentage of each. If the linen content is the

---

*a *slub* is a series of raised threads running across the warp.

1

biggest percentage the label will read linen/cotton.

*Repp*  A ribbed weave with thin and thick threads forming lines. Comes in a wide variety of plain colours. Made in cotton, rayon, silk, and wool (*wool* repp is not suitable for curtains).

*Sateen*  Used only for curtain lining, this is a fine woven fabric with a slight sheen on the right side. Mainly made in white or beige as these are the most practical shades. Colours are available, but make sure they are colour fast. Made in cotton.

*Satin*  A lustrous shiny fabric made both in heavy and light weights. Drapes very well. Best fibres for curtains are either silk or cotton, also made in rayon and a mixture of made-made fibres.

*Tapestry*  A multi-coloured fabric which is often designed to imitate wool embroidery. Made in cotton, wool and man-made fibre mixes. The lighter weights in this fabric are best for curtains.

*Towelling*  A looped pile cloth, used mainly in bathrooms as it absorbs the steam. Made of cotton, it can be patterned or plain.

*Velour*  One of the favourite fabrics for lined curtains, it is a pile cloth, made in various qualities, and a large range of colours. Most manufacturers recommend that the pile should brush *up*. This gives a much deeper and richer colour. The pile will fill out gradually and will appear thicker this way up. Make sure when you choose velour that it is held up the way it is going to be made up, otherwise it could look an entirely different shade. Made in cotton, silk and rayon.

## Fabrics to choose for loose covers

*Chintz*  This would not prove very hard wearing, and would need lining. Most suitable for bedroom chairs.

*Damask* (cotton)  Most suitable are the medium wearing qualities.

*Folk weave*  Closely woven type best for covers. Cotton and mixtures are suitable.

*Linen*  Very popular, hard wearing fabric, ideal for loose covers.

*Linen union*  Slightly cheaper than linen and also hard wearing.

*Repp*  Inclined to become greasy with wear on the arms of chairs. Cotton repp is the most suitable. Rayon repp is *not* strong enough for loose covers.

*Tapestry* (Cotton and man-made)  A medium weight is suitable for loose covers, the heavy-weight and wool tapestries are suitable for upholstery.

*Weave*  Rather a loose term to cover tweeds, and coarser woven fabrics. Many are made of cotton, or man-made fibres. Needs to be closely woven to wear well for loose covers. It makes loose covers look more like upholstered furniture, as it clings well to the underneath fabric.

## Fabrics to choose for bedcovers and cushions

*Brocade*  All types.

*Chintz*  See above.

*Damask*  All types.

*Dupion*  All types.

*Gingham*  For a child's room, fresh looking and easily laundered.

*Folk weave*  Better suited to a fitted bedcover, as it is too thick to pleat or gather. Ideal in a bed-sitting room.

*Linen* or *linen union*.

*Sateen*  Used to line bedcovers, and make inside covers for cushions (downproof

cambric must be used if the filling is feather or eiderdown).

*Satin* Cotton satin is the most suitable and most hard wearing type.

*Printed cotton* Ideal, looks crisp and is easily laundered.

*Cotton and polyester* Ideal to make matching bed bases, for duvets and pillows.

## Care of fabrics
When choosing a fabric for soft furnishing, bear in mind whether it will wash or dry clean and still maintain its good looks.

**Unlined curtains** This type of curtain is usually made in a washable fabric. Before washing, take out the hooks, loosen cords if necessary, and pull the heading tape out until it lies flat. Wash carefully following instructions on the care label. Iron up and down the length, not across.

**Lined curtains** These are better dry cleaned as they are less likely to shrink during cleaning than with washing. The two different types of fabric used together in lining a curtain, makes them more vulnerable to shrinkage as both fabrics have a different shrinkage level. Most lined curtains are very heavy, especially when wet, which is another reason why dry cleaning is preferable. The exception would be a cotton curtain, lined in cotton. These will wash successfully, and the colours remain brighter than when dry cleaned. When nearly dry, the curtains should be pressed with a hot iron up and down the length, *never* across the width as this will make the curtain misshapen.

Velour curtains will last for several years before they first need cleaning, if they are taken down and hung out of doors for a few hours, and then brushed or vacuum cleaned before being rehung. Although expensive to buy, velour will outlast many other fabrics, and can be dyed and relined long after its first youth. Several dry cleaning firms now have a home cleaning service, which means they will clean the curtains at the house, or will collect, clean and rehang the curtains

in the minimum time possible. This service is very useful if the curtains are interlined or very heavy.

**Loose covers** These need more frequent laundering, because the dirt is rubbed in and acts as an abrasive, so that the covers wear out more quickly. Covers can generally be washed, providing the washing instructions are carefully followed. Just before the covers are dry, press them and put them back on the chairs. This will enable them to stretch back to shape. The tuck-in must be thoroughly dry before tucking into the chair. If the fabric has to be dry cleaned, do not leave the covers folded up for too long afterwards, shake out the folds and fit the covers on. Most surface creases will disappear after a few hours in a warm room. Any creasing that persists can be pressed on the chair, by laying a length of cloth over the crease, so that the iron does not come in direct contact with the cover. This prevents shine on the fabric.

**Net Curtains** Nets should be washed frequently, in warm soapy water or a detergent. Man-made fibres can be drip-dried. Natural fibres or mixtures of both may need pressing with a cool iron.

## Care labelling
The Home Laundering Consultative Council have devised a system of labelling which gives the method of laundering recommended for different types of fabric. These labels are reproduced on washing powder and detergent packets, and on the settings on washing machines and irons. Many retailers supply these labels when fabric is sold. It is important to note the content of fabric when buying (see *Types of fabric*).

*Examples of the HLCC code appear overleaf*

The following are labels reproduced from the HLCC leaflet.

## Summary of washing symbols

| Symbol | Washing temperature | | Fabric | Benefits |
| | Machine | Hand | | |
| --- | --- | --- | --- | --- |
| **1** / 95 | very hot (95°C) to boil | hand hot 50°C or boil | White cotton and linen articles without special finishes | Ensure whiteness and stain removal |
| **2** / 60° | hot 60°C | hand hot 50°C | Cotton, linen or rayon articles without special finishes where colours are fast at 60°C | Maintains colours |
| **3** / 60° | hot 60°C | hand hot 50°C | White nylon; white polyester/cotton mixtures | Prolongs whiteness —minimises creasing |
| **4** / 50° | hand hot 50°C | hand hot 50°C | Coloured nylon; polyester; cotton and rayon articles with special finishes; acrylic/cotton mixtures; coloured polyester/cotton mixtures | Safeguards colour & finish—minimises creasing |
| **5** / 40° | warm 40°C | warm 40°C | Cotton, linen or rayon articles where colours are fast at 40°C, but not at 60°C | Safeguards the colour fastness |
| **6** / 40° | warm 40°C | warm 40°C | Acrylics; acetate and triacetate, including mixtures with wool; polyester/wool blends | Preserves colour & shape—minimises creasing |
| **7** / 40° | warm 40°C | warm 40°C | Wool, including blankets, and wool mixtures with cotton or rayon; silk | Keeps colour, size and handle |
| **8** / 30° | cool 30°C | cool 30°C | Silk and printed acetate fabrics with colours not fast at 40°C | Prevents colour loss |
| **9** / 95 | very hot (95°C) to boil | hand hot 50°C or boil | Cotton articles with special finishes capable of being boiled but requiring drip drying | Prolongs whiteness, retains special crease resistant finish |

Do NOT machine wash

Do NOT wash

### Washing temperatures

| | | |
| --- | --- | --- |
| 100°C | Boil | Self-explanatory. |
| 95°C | Very hot | Water heated to near boiling temperature. |
| 60°C | Hot | Hotter than the hand can bear. The temperature of water coming from many domestic hot taps. |
| 50°C | Hand-hot | As hot as the hands can bear. |
| 40°C | Warm | Pleasantly warm to the hand. |
| 30°C | Cool | Feels cool to the touch. |

## Dry cleaning

The letter in the circle refers to the solvent which may be used in the dry cleaning process, and those using coin operated dry cleaning should check that the cleaning symbol shown on the label is the same as that in the instructions given on the front of the machine.

 Goods normal for dry cleaning in all solvents.

 Goods normal for dry cleaning in perchloroethylene, white spirit, Solvent 113 and Solvent 11.

 May be dry cleaned professionally. Do not 'coin-op' clean.

 Goods normal for dry cleaning in white spirit or Solvent 113.

 Do not dry clean.

## Bleaching

 This symbol indicates that household (chlorine) bleach could be used. Care must be taken to follow the manufacturer's instructions.

 When this symbol appears on a label household bleach must *not* be used.

## Ironing

The number of dots in the ironing symbol indicates the correct temperature setting—the fewer the dots the cooler the iron setting.

| Cool | warm | hot | do not iron |

4

# 2: Choosing a style for curtains

The style of curtains you choose for a particular room is very important. Some will help to make a small room look larger, others make a large room look cosier. Balance and proportion should always be borne in mind. It is worthwhile spending time choosing the style of curtains that will best suit your room—for after they are made you may have to live with them for a long time!

Basically, there are three different lengths and widths to choose from **1, 2, 3.**

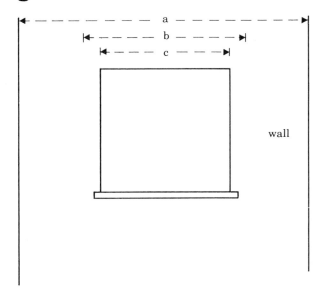

wall

**2** *Widths a) Recess width*
*b) 30 cm either side of the frame*
*c) Wall to wall*

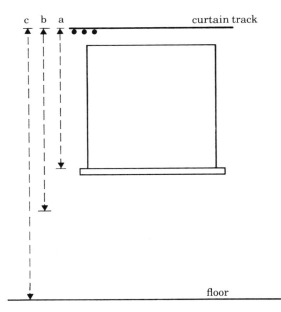

curtain track

floor

**1** *Lengths a) To the sill*
*b) 10 cm below the sill*
*c) To within 2 cm of the floor*

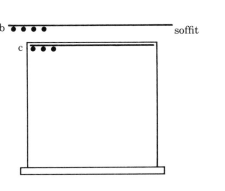

ceiling

soffit

**3** *Fitting the track or rod*
*a) From ceiling*
*b) From 10 cm above the soffit*
*c) Underside of soffit in recess*

5

The styles shown below are all for the same size window, which demonstrates the different effects that can be obtained. If the curtains are hanging from above the soffit, they must be balanced by the length below the sill or they will look top-heavy; 10 cm above and below is recommended, as curtains halfway between the sill and the floor look unbalanced (neither long or short) **4, 5, 6, 7, 8, 9.**

Individual windows need different treatments. Sometimes a radiator prevents the use of long curtains, or a favourite corner cabinet cannot be moved in order that the curtains may go wall to wall. Most ideas have to be adaptable to suit the needs of the surroundings and the financial circumstances.

**4** *This treatment with the curtains inside the recess makes the window small and dark*

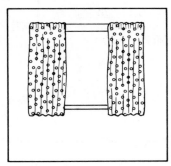

**5** *Measured above the soffit and below the sill, the track is wider than the window opening. This allows maximum light but still uses a relatively small amount of fabric*

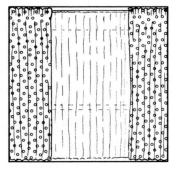

**6** *Curtains covering the whole wall area. This is an expensive way to curtain a room and can only be really effective if the net curtain is dense enough to disguise the shape of the window. It is ideal for patio or french doors when used without the net.*

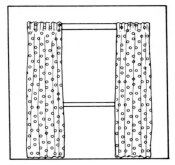

**7** *This window is measured from above the soffit to the floor, with the track wider than the window opening. This gives the room height, but looks unbalanced when the curtains are drawn back to expose the window*

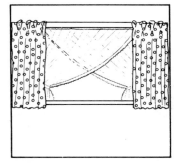

**8** *Track wall to wall, 10 cm above soffit and curtains falling to 10 cm below the sill. This treatment gives the maximum width, can be used with or without the nets and is most effective with this type of window*

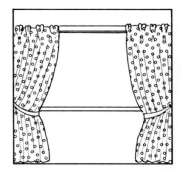

**9** *If long curtains are chosen for this type of window, they need to be balanced with the width. The tie-backs break the line of vision across the sill and give a softer draped effect*

## Proportion

It is most important when choosing a style to obtain the correct proportion; this applies particularly when deciding on a pelmet or valance. Here is a general guide to pelmet depths:

| Curtain length | Pelmet depth |
| --- | --- |
| 1 metre | 12.50 cm |
| 2 metres | 25.00 cm |
| 3 metres | 37.50 cm |

This measurement is the equivalent of an eighth of the total curtain measurement. If the pelmet is shaped, the above measurement would apply to the deepest part.

Soft curved lines are generally used in the more traditional style of window treatment. Square or straight lines blend with a modern type of décor. Swags and tails are used with traditional furnishings; these need to have a tall window to gain the maximum effect. Swags are usually made one quarter of the curtain length, and tails approximately a third of the curtain length at the deepest point of the tail. These are approximate measurements only, a good deal depends on personal choice and the size of the window.

*Curtain length balanced above and below the window*

*A large pattern is more effective when used for floor length curtains*

## Colour

Colour plays an important part in designing a room. Shades varying between yellow, orange, pink and red, will give a room a warm appearance; use these shades in a north facing room. Blue, mauve, grey and black or white will give a room a cool appearance and can be used to good effect in a room with a sunny aspect. Greens and browns fall in between these categories, and will blend with most shades; as they are nature's most predominant colours they make a good background. Too many colours in a room will overcrowd it, a blend of shades of the same colour will give a much better effect.

Here are three different types of colour scheme:

*Monochromatic*  One main colour is chosen, and varying shades of the same colour are used with it. By using fabrics and wall coverings of different textures, an interesting and restful effect can be achieved.

*Analogous* This scheme uses related colours, eg blue/green, blue, green, chartreuse, and yellow.

*Complementary* Use a dominant colour, eg orange, and complement it with a cool colour, eg blue. Use the two colours in a third to two thirds proportion to balance the scheme.

These schemes give a general guide line; the way to start your colour scheme is to choose the basic colour that pleases you and build on from that.

## Patterns and textures

When using a fabric with a large design (over 75 cm) make sure that at least two repeats of the pattern will be seen; an area from floor to ceiling is necessary to give the design its full impact. In a small room a very large design can be overpowering. A large design on a loose cover is fine, as long as the design fits into the area covered by the inside back of a chair. A design can be completely spoiled if the outer edges are cut away. Do not mix two different patterns, even if the colouring is similar; both patterns will lose their importance. Use the pattern as a focal point and blend the rest of the background with it.

Manufacturers are now making plain and patterned fabrics to mix and match, and many have wallpapers to match as well. This, of course, is taking a great deal of the guesswork out of furnishing. Small all-over designs are very popular with all age groups. Many are two-colour designs and are very easy to live with. As most of these are printed designs on cotton or cotton mixtures, they are particularly useful for bedroom furnishings, for example bed bases and duvet covers which need frequent laundering.

Stripes are popular from time to time, and it is nearly always possible to find a striped fabric in some form. Stripes running vertically will give height to a window, running horizontally they will give an appearance of width. Avoid extreme fashion in furnishing fabrics unless you are able to completely refurnish every few years (which will be unlikely!). Extreme designs or colours can soon pall and they date very quickly.

Plain or textured fabrics give a feeling of space, as they appear to make a room larger. Each type of fabric produces a different effect: plain fabrics reflect light, whereas a textured fabric absorbs light and appears heavier. Curtains look very elegant in a plain fabric, and enhance the look of a decorative track or rod. Plain curtains or covers can be trimmed with fringe or braid and some beautiful and individual effects can be achieved.

# 3: Curtain tracks

The first thing to decide when purchasing a curtain track is the type best suited to your purpose. There are a wide variety of tracks available, which can be purchased at most ironmongers, departmental stores, and DIY shops. The choice depends on where the track is to be fitted, what weight of curtain it has to hold, and whether it is going to be hidden behind a pelmet or valance, or be a decorative rail with an attractive heading on the curtain (for example, pinch pleats).

Having decided what type of rail is needed it must then be decided where, and by what method, it is to be fixed. A decorative rail is Rawlplugged to the wall using the brackets provided. These brackets are not visible from the front when the track is in place. Standard type track can be Rawlplugged to the wall but it is much better to fix it to a wooden lath or pelmet board as it gives better clearance at the back of the curtain heading, so preventing dragging against the wall. Fitting curtain rails is a job for an expert, and it usually pays in the end to have a professional to do it, particularly if the rail needs to be corded.

However, many people nowadays have good tool kits and are well able to tackle this type of job, if the fitting directions supplied with the rail are carefully followed. If fitting

*Swish Deluxe Imperial track*      *Photo: Swish*

standard track, sand-paper and paint the lath or pelmet board before fixing. Mark the holes to be drilled on the lath or board and drill holes right through the wood. Hold it in position on the wall (this usually calls for an assistant) and mark the wall by pushing a bradawl through the holes in the wood. Having marked all the holes, make sure they are running parallel with the ceiling and floor, then drill and Rawlplug the wall and proceed to fix the lath or board. The lath is usually fixed at least 8 cm above the soffit. If it is fixed lower down it can break the edge of the plaster, as several holes have to be drilled to take the Rawlplugs and screws **10.**

**10** *Lath fixed to wall*

**11** *Pelmet board fixed with brackets*

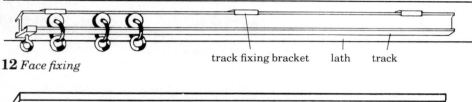

**12** *Face fixing*

track fixing bracket    lath    track

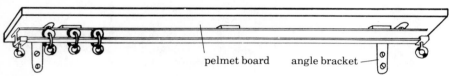

pelmet board    angle bracket

**13** *Top fixing*

If the pelmet board is supporting heavy curtains or if it is more than a metre wide, it is necessary to have support brackets at intervals of approximately 50 cm **11**.
The track can be fixed with wood screws onto the lath once it has been placed firmly on the wall. This type of fixing is called *face fixing* **12**.

The track may be fitted under the wood on the pelmet board, with wood screws, once the pelmet board has been securely fixed to the wall. This is called *top fixing* **13**.
It is better to overlap the track if possible, as this prevents the curtains 'gaping' at the top when drawn together. However, it is not always necessary to use two separate tracks, as most tracks have an overlap master runner **14, 15**.

Many tracks are now telescopic and can be pulled out to fit the size required. The fittings are already threaded, and some are available already corded. The fittings and the cording set does have to be adjusted to fit the window size however, so read the instructions carefully.

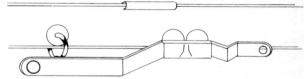

**14** *Overlap master runner*

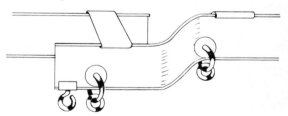

**15** *Two lengths of track used to make an overlap*

Tracks fall into approximately four categories, and although different manufacturers vary the type of fittings and finishes, they look very much alike.

### Standard track
Made in metal, nylon or plastic. Runners or gliders available for standard tracks are mostly made from nylon, although on the

heavier duty tracks metal runners are still available **16**.

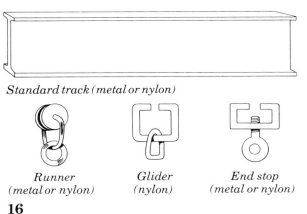

*Standard track (metal or nylon)*

*Runner (metal or nylon)*  *Glider (nylon)*  *End stop (metal or nylon)*

**16**

## Extending track

KIRSCH do a very good range of extending tracks, they are sold ready to fit and are internally corded. Buy the nearest size to your window measurements, not forgetting to add at least 15 cm extra each side, so that the curtains can be drawn well back from the window.

In the KIRSCH range, the types include *Swanglide* for lightweight curtains, *Regular* for both medium and heavy weight curtains, and *Double duty* for heavy curtains. All these tracks are stove enamelled white, and come ready-corded for a two-way draw, that is for two curtains. They can be adjusted for a one-way draw, either right or left handed. *Double duty* and *Regular* can be bent to fit round bay windows **17**.

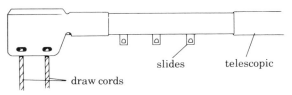

slides    telescopic

draw cords

**17** *Extending track*

## Decorative tracks

The SWISH *De luxe* track is included under this heading, because it is one of the many tracks that can be used without a pelmet to hide the

mechanism. It is a very neat unobtrusive type of track and is one of the strongest and most versatile of its type. The track is white plastic, with gliders that can be inserted after the rail has been fitted. This is most useful as extra gliders can be added without removing the end stops. This track can be curved round a bay window, and it can, on a straight run, be corded successfully **18**.

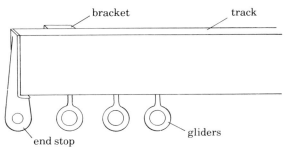

bracket    track

end stop    gliders

**18** *Swish de luxe track*

*Trimtrack*, manufactured by RUFFLETTE, is a similar type of track. The gliders run in a channel at the base of the track. This type can be corded and it is made in white plastic **19**.

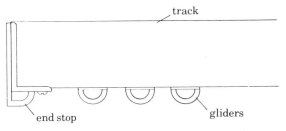

track

end stop    gliders

**19** *Trimtrack*

HARRISON *Drape* is another in this type of decorative track. It is made in aluminium and

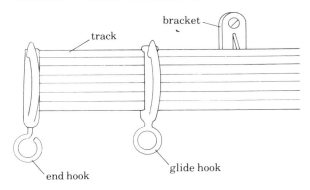

bracket

track

end hook    glide hook

**20** *Harrison Drape*

is available in silver. *Super drape* has a gold finish. The brackets and gliders are nylon. This track can be used on bay windows or straight windows. The glide hooks make it unnecessary to use hooks, as the glide hook will fit into the pockets of a pleating tape. Provision is there, however, for hooks to be used if desired. Detachable linings can be hooked on behind the curtain **20.**

## Decorative rods and cornice poles

HARRISON, KIRSCH, RUFFLETTE and SWISH, all make their own version of these rods or tracks. In recent years these decorative rods have become very popular. Most of the modern versions are hollow inside. This hollowed-out centre houses all the mechanism needed to make the track operate smoothly. From the front the rods look like solid poles with complete rings running along them. They are very efficient and neat, as they are usually corded internally. Most of these rods are telescopic. This means that a rod can be purchased and fitted immediately in most cases. The exceptions to the rule are naturally very large sizes or special orders. If the rod is not adjustable most stores will take the order and have a rod cut to size. Rods and poles are available in wood, plastic and metal finishes,

they can be plain, ribbed, round or square; all have immitation rings **21.**

Solid cornice poles have become popular again. This was one of the traditional ways of hanging a curtain. The poles can be bought in metal or wood and have to be cut if a special size is required. The rings on these poles are whole rings and they have no other mechanism. The curtains are drawn by hand. Wooden poles can be painted to match the décor of the room or stained to match the furniture **22.**

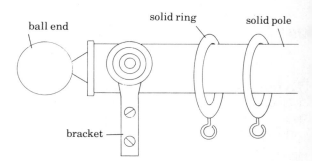

**22** *Cornice pole*

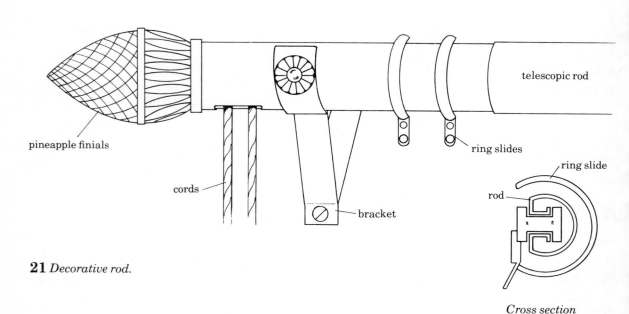

**21** *Decorative rod.*

*Cross section*

The following tracks are made by Antiference and sold under the brand name KIRSCH **23, 24, 25, 26, 27, 28, 29, 30, 31, 32, 33, 34.**

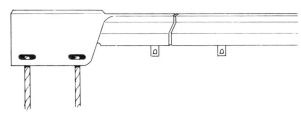

**23** *Swanglide medium weight, can be corded and is telescopically adjustable*

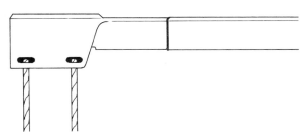

**24** *Superfine heavier weight, available in four sizes, telescopically adjustable. Two other rails in this range are Regular and Double Duty, both made to measure in straight runs or shaped to fit a bay window*

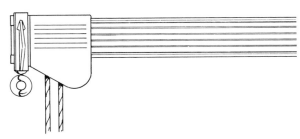

**25** *Decorail plastic, made in white or gold*

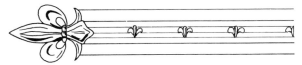

**26** *Black Prince Decorail with optional silver finials*

**27** *Decorail 2000 in silver aluminium for heavier curtains. Can be corded*

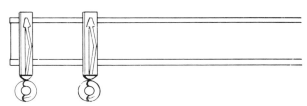

**28** *Monorail in white or white with gold trim*

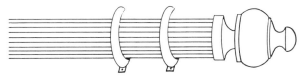

**29** *Sherwood, a mellow wood finish in two adjustable corded lengths*

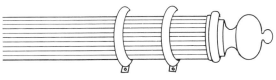

**30** *Vintage Alumigold or antique gold. Four corded lengths, fully adjustable*

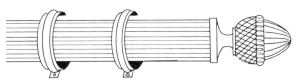

**31** *Chateau in antique white or brass, corded and adjustable lengths*

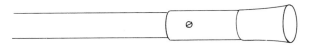

**32** *Decor glide in bright brass. In three adjustable lengths, all corded*

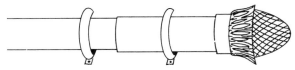

**33** *Golden glide brass finish. Four lengths, adjustable and corded*

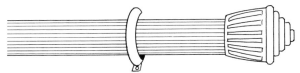

**34** *Continental in Alumigold. Approximately 4 cm in diameter it is cut to length and can be corded or uncorded*

The following tracks are made by Harrison-Beacon Limited and marketed under the name HARRISON **35, 36, 37, 38, 39, 40, 41.**

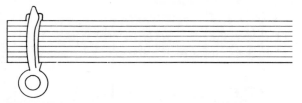

**35** *Drape, an aluminium track, siliconised for easy running. Used for straight or curved runs*

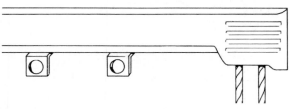

**36** *Monarch, an adjustable pre-corded metal track, finished in white*

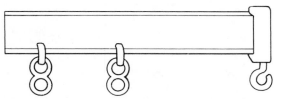

**37** *Glideway in white plastic with an invisible steel strip insert. Can be corded*

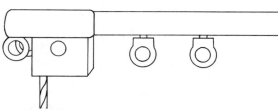

**38** *Neta made from silver anodised aluminium and siliconised for smooth running. Neta corded 960 twin track also in this range, has an overlap and integral cord control*

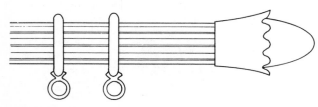

**39** *Cornice pole. A strong lightweight anodised aluminium cornice pole with matching finials. Available in six sizes and various lengths*

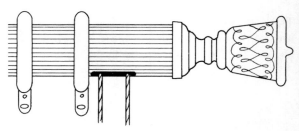

**40** *Marquis, a highly decorative pre-corded extending track, available in four sizes*

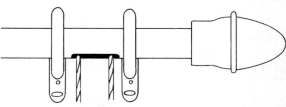

**41** *Ringslide, a plain gold coloured pole, is pre-corded and extendable. Available in four sizes.*

The following tracks are made by Thomas French and Company Limited, and are sold under the brand name RUFFLETTE **42, 43, 44.**

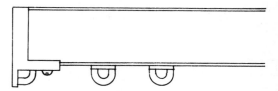

**42** *Trimtrack*

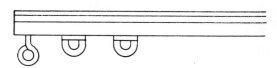

**43** *Sheerglide made in white plastic, for straight or curved runs*

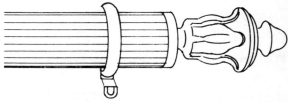

**44** *Classic is a decorative pole in anodised aluminium available in classic gold, classic silver and classic antique white, with choice of gold or white glider rings. Available with or without cord control mechanism*

The following tracks, manufactured by Swish Products Limited, are marked by the brand name SWISH **45, 46, 47, 48, 49, 50, 51.**

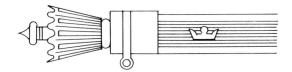

**50** *Finials for Sologlyde Regal in gold, for Sologlyde in white*

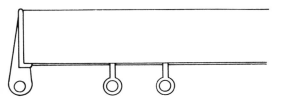

**45** *Swish de luxe made in white plastic for curved or straight runs, can be corded on straight runs only*

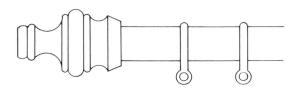

**51** *Swish wooden curtain pole in natural finish. Also available in walnut finish or white*

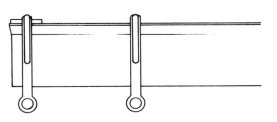

**46** *Sologlyde is a white plastic track, the glider hook can take a curtain and a separate lining. Sologlyde Regal has a gold band on the face of the track. Finials can be added to make an attractive finish to the ends*

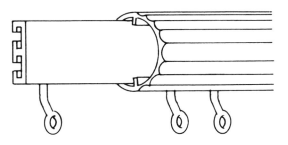

**47** *Imperial is a fluted trim that clips on to the Swish de luxe track. Available in gold or white*

**48** *Finials for de luxe Imperial in gold or white*

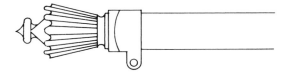

**49** *Finials for de luxe track in white or gold*

# 4: Heading tapes

There is also a confusing variety of heading tapes to choose from in the soft furnishing departments of shops and stores. Some require special hooks, others an absolutely specific amount of fabric to achieve the required effect and there are also those that are unsuitable for some kinds of tracks or rods.

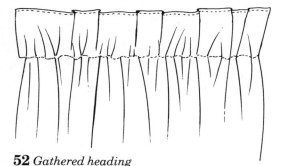

*52 Gathered heading*

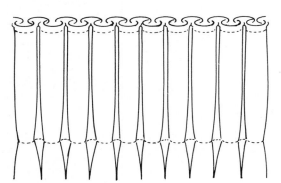

*53 Pencil pleats*

In *Types of Heading* (Chapter 7), methods of attaching tapes to the curtains are shown. The following are some of the heading tapes available, and the best type of track or rod to use with them **52, 53, 54, 55.**

*Standard* one-inch RUFFLETTE tape is available in a selection of colours to match the curtain

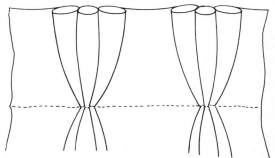

*54 Pinch pleats (or French pleats)*

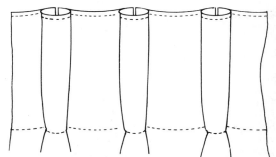

*55 Cartridge pleats*

fabric. It is generally used with standard track, behind a pelmet. This tape is also made in white polyester and can be used for lightweight curtains and net curtains **56.**

RUFFLETTE lining tape is used on detachable linings, see Chapter 5. Very simple to use, the tape has a double skirt at the lower edge trapping the lining in the centre. Once sewn in place it is gathered in the same way as the standard tape **57.**

Pencil pleating tape brand names include KIRSCH *Decortape*, SWISH *Deep pleat* tape and RUFFLETTE *Trident*. There are many variations from different manufacturers of this type of heading tape. Mostly it is made with three lines of pockets. This is very useful if you

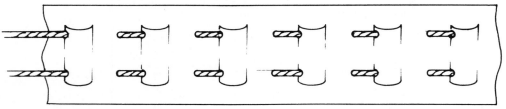

*56 Standard tape*

need to adjust the curtain length, or wish to have the heading higher or lower, above the track. This type of tape is approximately 8 cm deep. It is also made in Tervoil and Terylene **58**.

*Regis* pencil pleating tape is made by RUFFLETTE and has a row of pockets at one edge. The pockets are placed at the bottom of the heading, if the curtain is to cover the track. They are placed at the top, however, if the curtain is to hang below the track or pole. It is suitable for most types of curtain fabric. For lightweight or sheer fabrics Tervoil 60 tape should be used **59**.

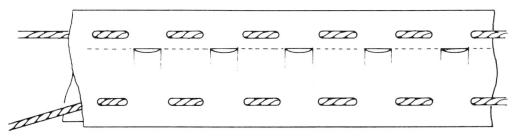

**57** *Lining tape*

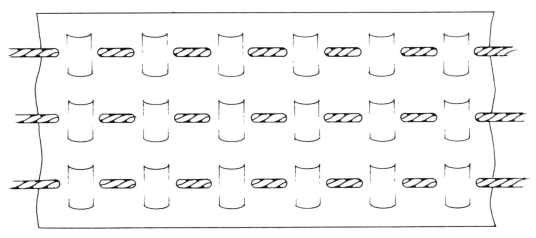

**58** *Pencil pleating tape*

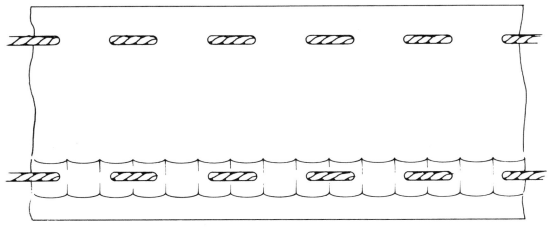

**59** *Rufflette Regis tape*

Pinch pleated heading tape. Several types of these tapes are available, but some of them need special hooks so find out about this before making your purchase. The plain pocketed type of tape without draw strings is the type used with three pronged hooks. See Chapter 7 for this type of heading **60.** This tape is approximately 8 cm deep.

Automatic pleating tape brand names include RUFFLETTE *Tridis, Tridis 40* and *Cartridge pleat* tape. These tapes allow the pleats to be placed automatically when the draw cords are pulled up to their full extent. This type of tape has special hooks to keep the pleats in place (R10). The *Tridis* range is for triple pleats, and the *Cartridge pleat* tape is for a single pleat. Twice the length of the track must be allowed when calculating the amount of fabric needed.

The depth of the pleating tape is approximately 4 cm (*Tridis 40*) or 8 cm (*Tridis* and *Cartridge*). For a deeper triple pleat heading another tape *Tridis 140* has been introduced, which gives a depth of approximately 14 cm **61.**

Cartridge pleats. Tapes now available from RUFFLETTE to make cartridge pleats automatically are available in two versions. *Underslung* cartridge for use when the heading hangs below a decorative pole; *standard* cartridge for use on ordinary track where the curtain heading covers the track. This tape is made in white synthetic fabric, and can be used on sheer or solid materials. After the curtain heading has been pulled to size, the pleats can be filled with tissue, or a roll of fine buckram or Vilene. This gives the pleats a rounded look. The padding, of

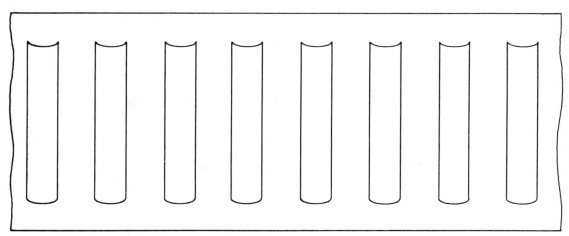

**60** *Kirsch Easypleat, pinch pleat tape for use with three pronged hooks*

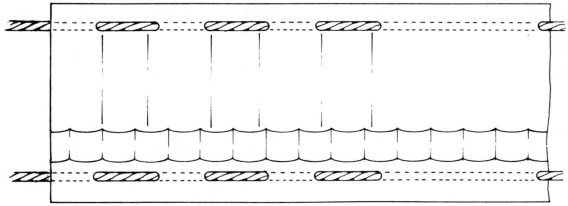

**61** *Automatic pleating tape*

course, must be removed for cleaning. The fabric required for this type of heading is twice the length of the curtain track.

On almost every type of tape, the standard type of hook can be used. Only the pinch pleating tapes need special hooks, and these are usually bought in kit form, complete with the length of tape required. Tapes and extra hooks can both be purchased separately 62, 63, 64, 65, 66, 67, 68.

Standard one prong hooks are made in nylon, solid brass, aluminium and plastic. They are used with all standard tapes and most pencil pleats. Nylon and plastic hooks are used also for net curtains 62, 63.

*62 Standard one prong hook, nylon or plastic*

*63 Standard one prong hook, brass or aluminium*

Two prong hooks are made in chrome plated metal. They are used with pinch pleat tape to hold pleats secure. *Tridis* and *Cartridge* by RUFFLETTE are used with these hooks 64.

*64 Two prong hook*

Three prong hooks are used with KIRSCH *Easypleat tape*. They are made of chrome plated metal and can have long or short necks. Using the short-necked pins raises the curtain above the rail 65, 66.

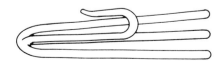

*65 Three pronged hook with short neck*

*66 Three pronged hook with long neck*

Pin hooks are made of chrome plated metal. Very useful hooks, they can be pinned in position to raise or lower a curtain. Pin hooks are used with hand sewn pinch pleats and any standard or pencil pleating tape. Short or long necked hooks are available 67.

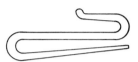

*67 Pin hook*

Sew-on hooks, made in solid brass are used for hand headed and very heavy curtains 68.

*68 Sew-on hook*

# 5: Measuring and estimating curtains

Incorrect measuring and estimating the amount of fabric required can be a very expensive mistake. All kinds of factors such as the fullness required, and repeating patterns on the fabric, have to be considered.

To measure for curtains where the rail shows above the top of the curtain, first measure from eye of rail to length required (eg to sill or floor). Then measure width of rail allowing 15 cm extra for overlap **69**.

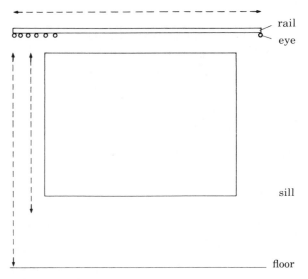

**69** *Measuring a window for curtains with standard heading*

This type of curtain has a gathering tape sewn to the top edge. The curtain and rail are normally covered by a pelmet or valance. To estimate the amount of fabric required, take the measurement of the length. Add to this measurement an allowance for hems (15 cm). This will give the overall cut length.

To find how many widths of fabric are needed to cover the width of the window, work out how many pieces of fabric at 122 cm it will take to cover the width of the window. For example, if a window is 2.40 m wide it will

need two widths of fabric 1.22 m wide to cover it. Most curtains need at least one and a half times the width of the window to give the fullness required. However, whenever possible I would recommend double fullness as it greatly improves the drape of the curtains. (For example for a window 2.40 m wide, one and a half times the fullness requires three widths. Twice the fullness needs four widths).

After deciding how many widths of fabric to use, multiply this by the overall cut length. (For example four widths of fabric multiplied by a cut length of 2.15 m = 8.60 m).

When the fabric is plain, the lengths are cut one after the other leaving no waste. However, when using patterned fabric the pattern repeat must be allowed for when estimating. The waste section is added to the overall cut length when calculating the amount **70**.

If the curtain is going to cover the top of the track, and with modern decorative rails this is necessary, the extra measurement should be added to the overall cut length. When estimating fabric remember that a curtain with a pencil pleat heading needs to be at least twice as wide as the window area, while a pinch pleated curtain should contain at least two and a half times the width of the same area.

## Cutting out and making unlined curtains

Lay the fabric right side up on a flat, square table. Keep the selvedges level with the table edge and make sure the cut end is square to the selvedges but, if you have a large pattern and it is printed slightly off square, it is much better to have the pattern running straight rather than the fabric exactly square, nothing offends the eye more than a pattern running downhill! **71**.

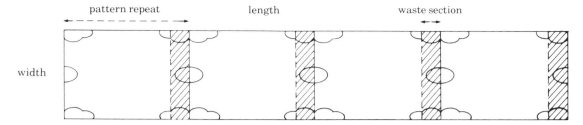

**70** *Cutting out patterned fabric*

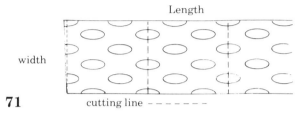

**71**

After cutting all the lengths, the fabric has to be pinned and joined together. Lay the fabric right sides together, pinning $1\frac{1}{2}$ cm from side edges. If the selvedge is tight, cut it off completely. If it is flat, snip the edge at intervals of 15 cm all the way up the sides. This enables the seams to lie flat as tight selvedges are one of the major causes of puckering. Machine along the pin line, taking out the pins as you progress. Hold the fabric between thumb and forefinger, either side of the foot, keeping fabric taut **72**.

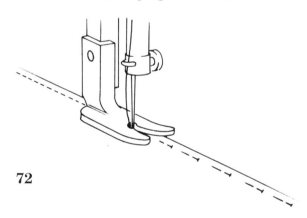

**72**

Measure off the first length and mark with chalk. Check the overall measurement then cut across the width. Use firm long strokes with the scissors, this prevents a ragged edge. If there is waste between the pattern repeat, cut it away. If it is left on the length it can cause confusion (you will come across one length longer than the others, and think you have cut all the other lengths short). Mark each length on the wrong side with a cross at the bottom left hand corner. If you do this as you cut each length you will save a lot of time trying to find out which way up each length should be (particularly with a pile or silk fabric).

*To make sure that the cut end is square to the selvedges cut it to the thread, that is, pull a thread across the fabric at right angles to the selvedge and cut along this line*

To make a flat seam, press the seam open, cut off one side to within ½ cm and turn the other side over ½ cm then over again. Tack this hem flat to the curtain, and slip stitch in place. Remove tacking and commence the side hems **73, 74.**

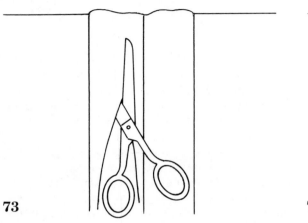

**73**

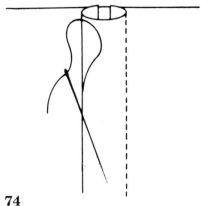

**74**

Half widths should be paired, and go to the outer edges of the window **75, 76.**

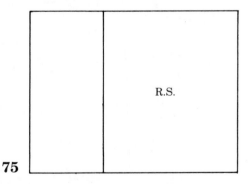

R.S.

**75**

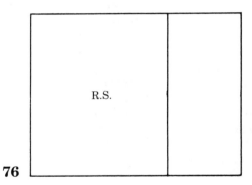

R.S.

**76**

Cut the selvedge edge off at the sides, and turn in ½ cm. Turn again, this time allowing 1½ cm. Pin in place and machine close to the edge of the inner fold. Machine both sides **77.**

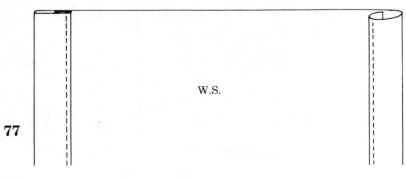

W.S.

**77**

Turn up the bottom hem to 5 cm, turn again
5 cm so that the hem is double. Pin into
position, keeping the thread line or pattern
straight. Machine straight across, fastening
the beginning and end securely **78.**

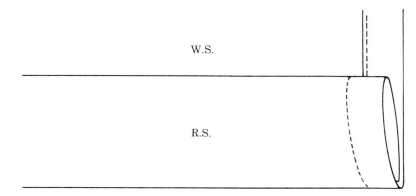

W.S.

R.S.

**78**

Slipstitch down the sides of the hem. This
method of making does not usually require
the corners to be weighted, as the fabric used
is washable **79, 80.**

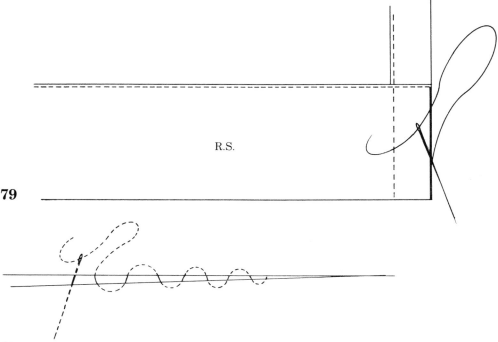

R.S.

**79**

**80** *Slipstitch detail*

Press the curtain with a steam iron if possible.
Press up and down the length on the wrong
side of the fabric. Do not press from side to
side as the fabric will go out of shape.

After pressing, remeasure the fabric to the finished length required, turn over the top and press down. The curtain is now ready to trim, before putting on the heading tape **81**.

Unless the curtains are going behind a pelmet, the tape is usually sewn approximately $2\frac{1}{2}$ cm down from the top of the curtain. This has to be allowed for when taking the overall measurement. If the curtain is to go under a pelmet the tape should be sewn right at the top. Trim curtain so that the raw edge will be covered by the heading tape **82**.

To attach the appropriate heading tape see Chapter 7.

## Detachable lining

A detachable lining can be made at the same time as, and used with, an unlined curtain, or they can be made to fit existing curtains. The advantage of this type of lining is that it can be unhooked from the curtain, and laundered separately. They do need to be caught at intervals down the sides, to prevent the curtain and lining from parting as this can look very untidy. The lining is made in exactly the same way as the unlined curtain. When you have made the lining up to the final measuring stage, check the

measurements against the curtain. Measure the curtain from the base of the tape to 2 cm above the bottom hem. This will give the exact measurement required for the lining **83**.

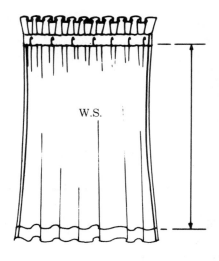

W.S.

**83**

Having measured the lining to the correct size, instead of folding the top down, as with the curtain, the lining should be cut straight across the measured line. The lining is now ready to have the tape attached. Detachable

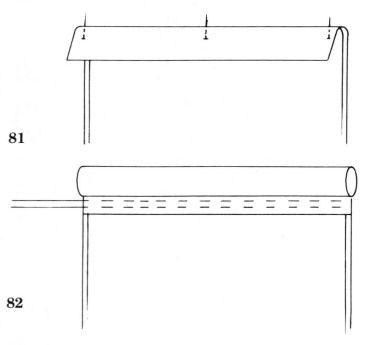

**81**

**82**

ining tape is made by RUFFLETTE especially for this purpose. The tape is double, so that the raw top edge of the lining can be inserted between the two sides of the tape **84.**

Pin and then machine the tape in place. Fold the raw edges of the tape in at each end. Leave the draw cords free at one end and secure the cords firmly at the other end. The lining can now be pulled up to fit the size of the curtain heading. This is done in exactly the same manner as for a curtain with a gathered heading (see Chapter 7). After pulling up the heading, secure the ends and

make a cleat. Insert the hooks, and the lining is now ready to be hooked to the curtain. The hooks from the lining are inserted into the pockets of the main curtain. Make sure they are in between the hooks that are already on the curtain, this will ensure that the linings do not interfere with the fixing of the curtain to the track **85.**

Hang the curtain complete with the lining, and catch the lining to the curtain at intervals of approximately 30 cm, keeping the lining approximately 2 cm from the side edge of the curtains to prevent it showing from the front.

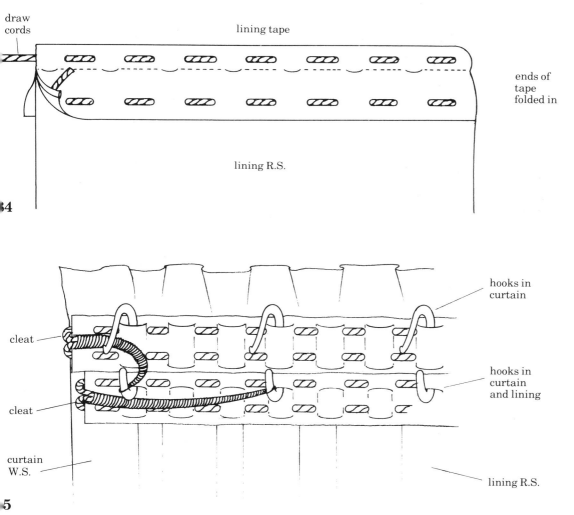

draw cords

lining tape

ends of tape folded in

lining R.S.

84

cleat

cleat

curtain W.S.

hooks in curtain

hooks in curtain and lining

lining R.S.

85

# 6: Lined curtains

Lined curtains hang well and, most important in a world running short of energy supplies, they help to keep in the heat in winter.

Estimate the amount of fabric needed, as for the unlined curtain in Chapter 5. Measure each length of lining 5 cm shorter than the curtain length. Cut off the lengths of fabric, and pin together ready to stitch by machine. (Remember to cut off the selvedges before joining). Cut off lengths of lining, and join in the same manner as the curtains. The selvedge edge on the lining is usually slack, and only needs to have the edges clipped. Turn up the hem on the lining $1\frac{1}{2}$ cm then 5 cm. Stitch in place by machine, using matching thread.

The next step is to hand stitch the curtain at sides and lower edge. Either a serging stitch or herringbone stitch can be used. Although this stitch is rather large, it is permanent, so it has to be sewn in a matching thread. The purpose of this stitch is to hold the sides flat, and thus stop them curling in towards the lining. Leaving the edge raw, turn the side in $3\frac{1}{2}$ cm. Starting approximately 12 cm from the lower edge of the curtain proceed to stitch up the side **86, 87**.

After serging both side hems, turn up the bottom hem. Turn in 5 cm then 5 cm again making a double hem. Press the side and bottom hems, creasing the edges sharply. Unfold the bottom hem. Fold the corner of the fabric across at an angle of 45°. Lining up the crease marks as shown in diagram, re-fold the sides and hem, thus forming a mitre **88, 89**.

Cover a lead weight with small circles of lining, sew round the outline and trim off excess fabric **90**.

Insert the weight into the corner and slipstitch in place. Slipstitch the hem, taking only a thread of the main fabric so that the stitches remain invisible on the right side. If the curtain has more than one width of fabric a weight must be inserted in the hem at each seamline **91**.

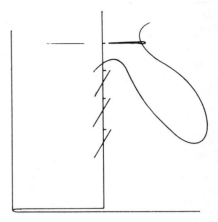

**86** *Stitch detail, serge stitch*

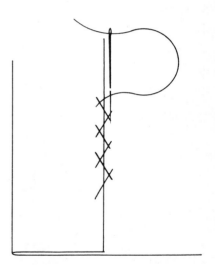

**87** *Stitch detail, herringbone stitch*

*Note* When working on velour or other pile fabrics the hem should be turned up to 8 cm and left flat. The edges are then herringbone stitched instead of slipstitched.

The mitred corner enables you to get rid of surplus fabric without cutting any away. This is particularly necessary if the curtains need to be let down at a later date. The mitre lies flat and gives a neat finish to a corner. The 45° mitre is usually used on curtains as well as other items of furnishing, for example, bedcovers.

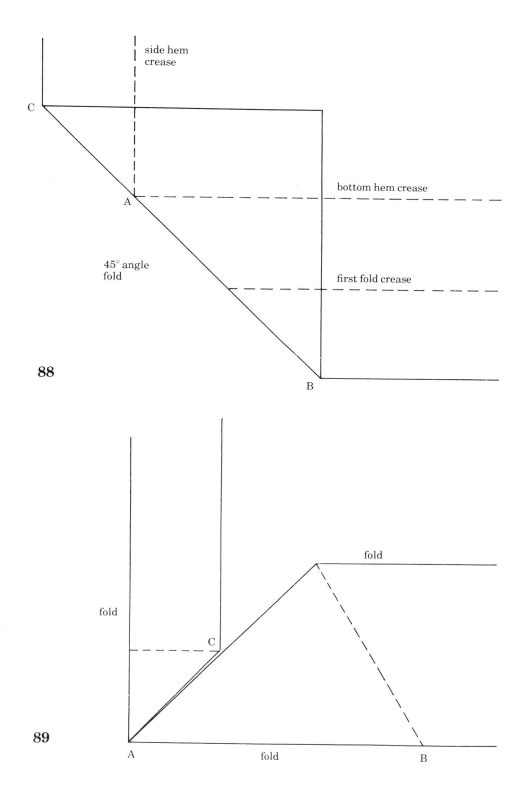

**88**

side hem crease

C

bottom hem crease

A

45° angle fold

first fold crease

B

**89**

fold

fold

C

fold

fold

A

B

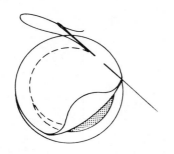

**90**

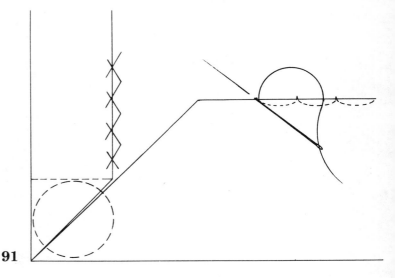

**91**

Press both the lining and the curtain on the wrong sides, pressing up and down the length, never from side to side. (When pressing a pile fabric (eg velour) press in one direction only, with the pile going down. Always press on the wrong side.) Lay the curtain right side down, square with the edge of the table. Place the lining on top, wrong sides together, making sure that the lining is paired with the curtain, that is, that the seams match. Place the lining 2 cm up from the lower edge of the curtain.

Turn the lining back down the whole length, starting at the middle seam. Lock stitch at intervals of approximately 20 cm all the length of the curtain, taking only a thread of the curtain fabric with each stitch. Repeat the locking process across the curtain on every half width of fabric. Make sure that the stitches are left slack, or they will pull the curtain when hanging and cause dragging **92, 93, 94.**

Trim the lining level with the side edges of the curtain, turn this raw edge under, leaving 2 cm of curtain showing. Tack the lining in place, keeping it slack against the curtain **95.**

Slipstitch in place, starting 7 cm along the hem of the lining. Remove tacking. Measure the curtain to the overall finished length. Turn over curtain and lining together at the top and press ready for the heading tape. Trim excess fabric and finish the heading as for unlined curtains (Chapter 5).

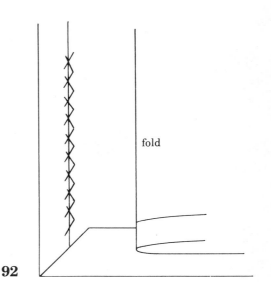

**92**

fold

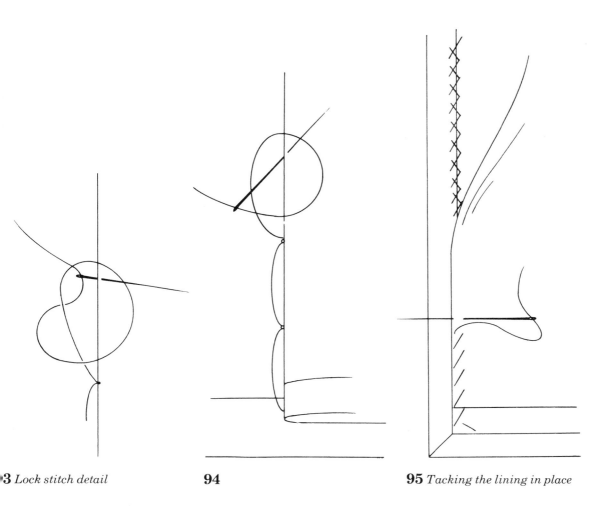

**93** *Lock stitch detail*      **94**      **95** *Tacking the lining in place*

# Interlined curtains

This type of curtain has an inner lining of bump, or dommette. This makes the curtain very heavy and gives a thick luxurious look to the outer fabric. It is used particularly for long curtains. One of the advantages is that it prevents light penetrating through the curtain, and also insulates the room when the curtains are drawn. The interlining (bump) should be cut to the same size as the curtain fabric. The fabric should be laid on the table right side down. The interlining is then placed on the fabric and smoothed out until it lies flat. The interlining is then turned back, and locked at each half width, as with lined curtains. If the fabric has to be joined to make up the width, make a seam and press open before applying the interlining. To make a seam on the interlining, overlap the selvedges by $1\frac{1}{2}$ cm and stitch in place with two parallel rows of machining. Alternatively seam with a single row of zigzag stitching. If the selvedge edge is tight cut it right away, as the seam must be as smooth as possible **96**.

Once the locking has been completed, treat the fabric and interlining as one, and turn the sides in 3 cm and serge in the same manner as for lined curtains. Serge both sides, then turn up the hem to a depth of 8 cm, mitre the corners and using a small stitch, slip-stitch in place. Insert covered

29

weights in the corners and on seam lines and secure in place. Sew the hem with a herring-bone stitch making sure that the stitch does not go through to the front surface **97**.

When the curtain is finally prepared, cut the lining to size and place with the wrong side facing the curtain. Then lock stitch at every half width. After locking, turn the sides and lower edge of the lining in until 2 cm of the main fabric is showing. Tack the lining in place and slipstitch all round **98**.

Check the finished measurement, turn down the top and trim ready for the heading. A hand heading is usually used on an interlined curtain.

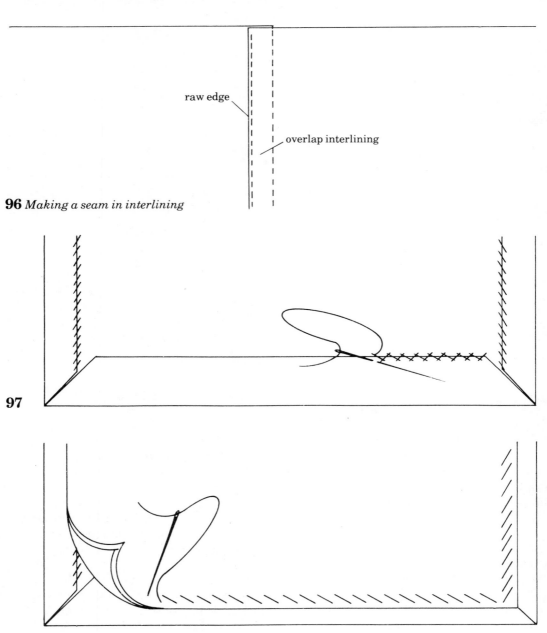

raw edge

overlap interlining

**96** *Making a seam in interlining*

**97**

**98** *Tacking the lining in place*

# 7: Adding the heading tape

Different kinds of heading tape require different treatments to achieve the right effect.

**A gathered heading**  Fold under about 1 cm at each end of the tape. Tuck under the end of the heading. Pin or tack in place. Machine in place, starting at the bottom left hand corner. Sew across the end and along the top edge. Start again at bottom left and stitch in the same direction as for the top edge. Leave the two strings loose at the beginning of the tape, but secure firmly at the other end. If the curtains have half widths, leave the strings out at the half width end **99.**

**99**

Tie a knot in the strings and loop them round a door handle or a stationary object. Pull the curtain heading right back (this sets the pleats) **100.**

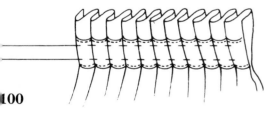

**100**

Divide the size of the rail, by the number of curtains to be hung from it. This will give you the heading measurement. Add 5 cm to allow for overlapping **101.**

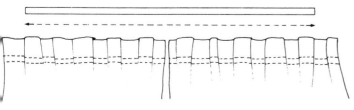

**101**

Ease the pleats along to the correct measurement. Tie off with a loop **102.**

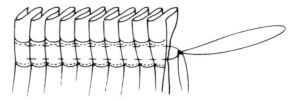

**102**

Wind excess string around the loop to make a cleat. This enables the curtain to be pulled flat again for laundering **103.**

**103**

Insert a hook in the end of the cleat and attach to the heading tape. Insert hooks along the length of tape approximately every 8 cm **104.**

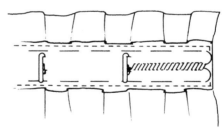

**104**

The curtains are now ready to hang. Remember that the half widths always go to the outside edge of the window frame.

**Pencil pleat tape**   This is is applied in the same way as the gathering tape. It is, however, advisable to have approximately 1½ cm of fabric above the tape. This gives a deeper heading and also stops the weight of the tape dragging the top forward and exposing the tape **105.**

After sewing on the tape, pull the curtain to size as for the gathered heading. Place the pleats in even, upright folds. Place the hooks in the pockets in the tape at intervals of 8 cm **106, 107.**

Finish with a cleat as for a gathered heading.

**Pinch pleat tape**   This is applied in the same way as the pencil pleat tape, however, the spaces for the hooks must be worked out to give the correct heading measurement. After sewing on the tape, start at the centre pocket and insert the middle prong of the triple hook.

Leave a gap of one pocket, and then insert the outer prongs. Continue along the length of the tape, leaving four pockets flat between each pinch pleat. To adjust the finished width, leave extra gaps between the pleats to lengthen, and allow less gap between pleats

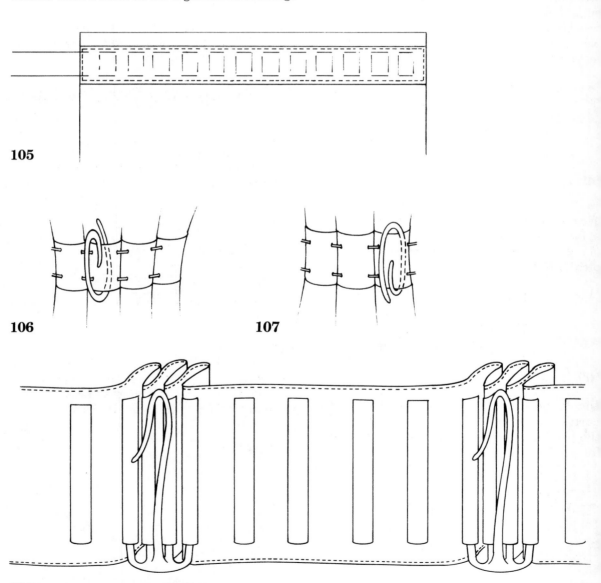

**105**

**106**          **107**

**108** *Pinch pleat tape using long neck hooks*

*Hand made pinch pleats with buckram*

to shorten. Allow at least 5 cm extra on each curtain as the weight tends to make them concertina **108.**

**Pinch pleats with buckram** (used on lined curtains). Pull back the lining from the top of the curtain. Insert 10 cm fusible buckram making sure it is in line with the top crease. Turn the top edge of the curtain over the buckram and iron in place. Fold the lining inwards to just below the top of the curtain and slipstitch in place. Turn the curtain so that the right side is towards you. Measure along the top, and mark the centre with a pin.

An average pleat would take about 13 cm with a 13 cm space between each pleat. Mark the pleats with pins **109.**

Fold the fabric at these marks and machine, or back stitch by hand, right through the fabric, buckram and lining for a distance of 10 cm (this should finish just below the buckram) **110.**

Any adjustment to the measurement of the width should be made at the pinning stage. Make the pleat smaller, rather than making the space larger, as the space will tend to droop forward if it is too wide.

After completing the first stage all along the heading, divide each pleat into three, by folding concertina fashion. Backstitch along the bottom, right through the three folds. Catch the top of the pleats, to hold them in place, with a small overlocking stitch. Complete by either using pin hooks on the back of each pleat or hand sewing long neck brass hooks, to each pleat, using a blanket stitch **111, 112.**

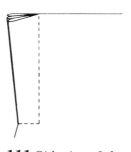  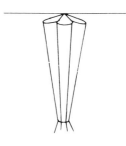

**111** *Side view of pleat*    **112** *Front view of pleat*

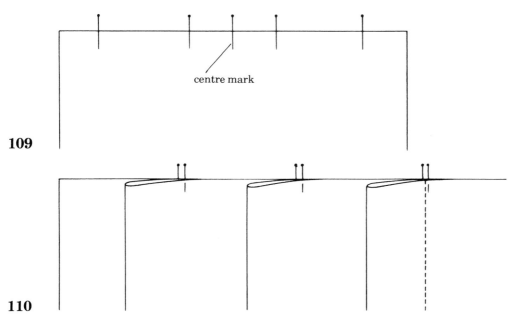

centre mark

**109**

**110**

**Hand heading** This type of heading can be used on lined or interlined curtains, as it is strong as well as decorative. When the curtain has been measured to the correct length, turn over at the top and trim to 3 cm. Measure across the width at the top edge, and mark with a pin halfway across, then divide again and mark the quarters **113.**

Cut a length of webbing to the *finished* size of the curtain, adding extra for turnings each end, also approximately 10% extra should be allowed for fabric taken up while stitching. After adding these measurements, cut to size and mark the webbing into half and quarters.

Cut a strip of lining approximately 10 cm in

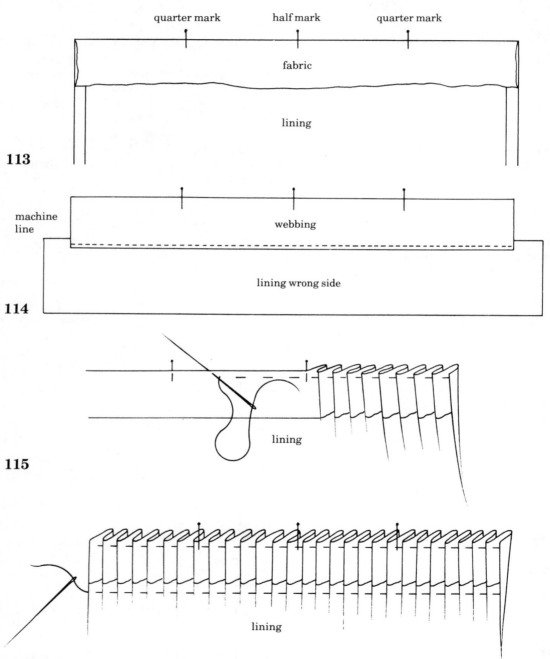

**116** *Both rows of gathers completed*

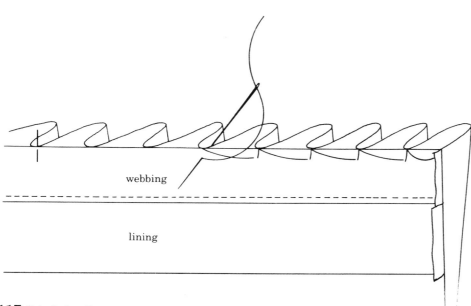

**117** *Stitch detail*

depth, and 4 cm longer than the length of webbing. Lay the webbing on the wrong side of the lining strip overlapping by 1½ cm. Leave 2 cm each end to turn in at a later stage. Machine along the edge of the webbing so that it is attached to the lining with a flat seam **114.**

Using a strong thread to match the main fabric, gather the curtain by hand, between each quarter mark. Pull up until it matches the quarter mark on the tape and fasten off on each section. This first line of stitching is along the top edge of the curtain. When this line is complete, measure from the top the same depth as the tape being used, and gather another line in quarters in exactly the same manner as before. It is very important that the stitches run exactly in line, as these stitches form the flutes which must stand upright **115, 116.**

Once both rows of gathers are complete, the strip of webbing with the lining attached must be pinned in place. This is done by matching the half and quarter marks. Even out the flutes and proceed to stitch in place (see stitch detail) **117.**

Stitch all along the top and fasten the ends securely. Working from the front of the

curtain place the flutes in an upright position, stitch right through the webbing on the bottom edge and secure each flute with a back stitch **118.**

When the bottom row of stitching is complete, turn the curtain and continue working on the back. The hooks must be sewn on at this stage, these are brass hooks with a long neck, set at intervals of 7 cm; these hooks are buttonhole stitched right through all the layers of material except the main fabric. Keep the hooks level along the bottom edge of the webbing **119.**

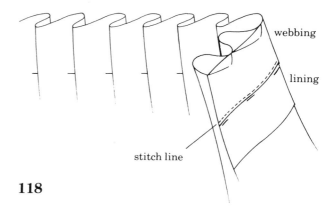

**118**

After sewing on all the hooks, turn the strip of lining up to cover the webbing and hooks, pin in position, and slipstitch all round. Turn in all the edges so that the top part of the hook is free **120.**

This heading can be made deeper, by leaving a heading of fabric above the webbing or using a much deeper webbing and sewing the hooks halfway up the webbing **121.**

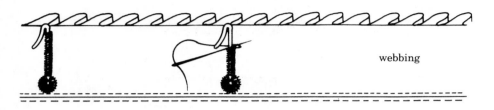

webbing

lining W.S.

**119** *Sewing on hooks*

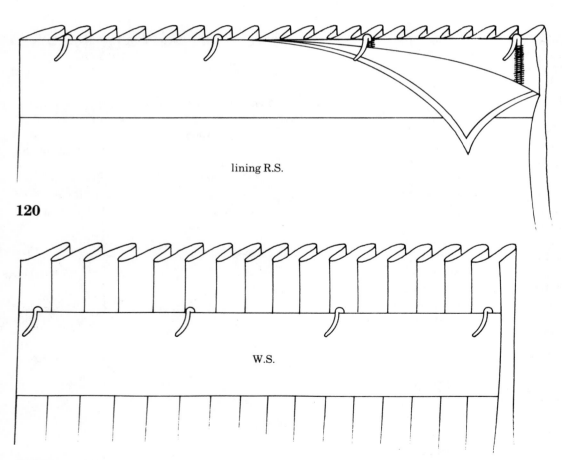

lining R.S.

**120**

W.S.

**121** *Deep heading*

# 8: Pelmets and valances

Pelmets and valances are a decorative way of covering the track and cording mechanism and finishing the top of the window. The kind you choose will depend on the style of your windows and curtains.

Made with buckram, they are permanently stiff. Buckram is cut to the desired shape and covered with fabric, either matching or contrasting with the curtains **122**.

Take the measurements along the width of the pelmet board, and allow extra for the returns. Decide on the depth and shape required, see Chapter 2 for suggested proportions **123, 124**.

The shallowest depth is usually one sixth of the depth of the pelmet, but this is variable because of differing designs. The shallow points should cover the track mechanism and the soffit **125**.

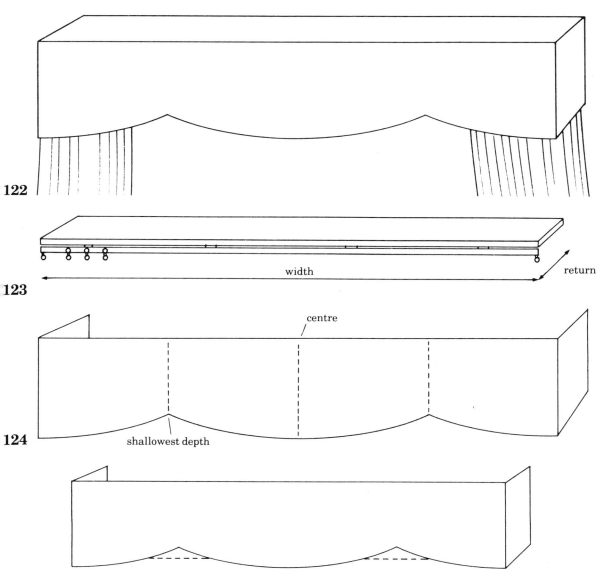

**122**

**123** width  return

**124** centre
shallowest depth

**125** *Pelmet incorrectly made, not covering soffit*

To design the pelmet, cut the length and depth required, on a length of paper. Do *not* add the returns at this stage as it will upset the proportion. Fold the paper in half, vertically. Divide the half section into five portions and draw on the design **126, 127.**

Cut out the design and add the return measurement. The design can now be transferred to the buckram. Draw round the

shape, include returns and cut out the buckram. The pelmet is now ready to cover with fabric.

Measure the depth of the pelmet and allow an extra 2 cm top and bottom for turnings. If the pelmet is wider than the width of material, you must place a complete width in the centre of the pelmet, stitch a piece of fabric at either side, and press flat.

Press the fabric, and place in position on the buckram. Pin top and bottom, starting at the centre, and smoothing the fabric towards the edges as you pin **128.**

Turn pelmet over and, with wrong side facing you, slightly dampen the edges of the buckram, by wiping with a damp cloth to a depth of 2 cm from the outside edge. Turn the edges of the fabric over to the back of the

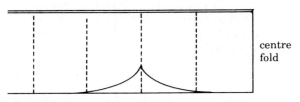

centre fold

**126** *Pelmet folded in half and divided into five sections. Front width* only, *returns not added*

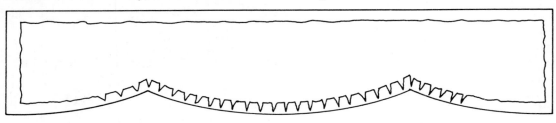

**127** *Complete pelmet front, no returns added*

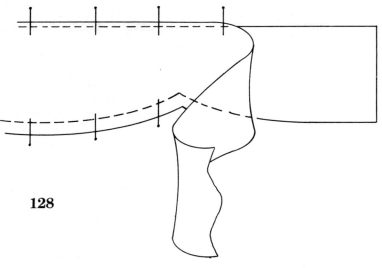

**128**

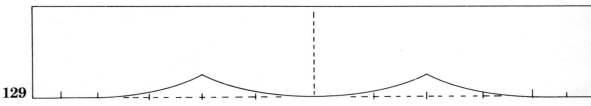

**129**

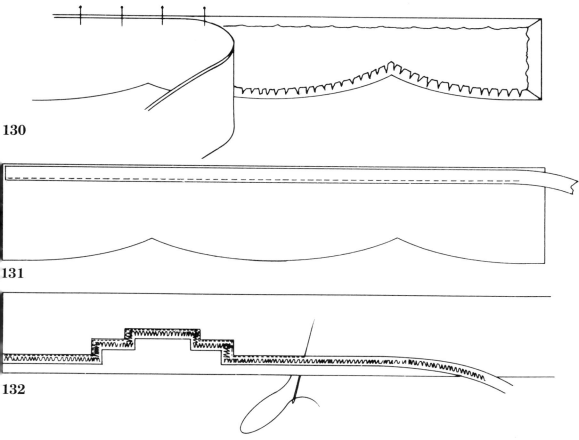

**130**

**131**

**132**

pelmet and using a warm iron, press hard until the fabric has stuck. To stick round the curved edges, snip the fabric to allow it to lie smoothly. If the pelmet is to be trimmed it must be done at this stage. (See *Trimming* below) **129.**

Cut and join the lining material in exactly the same way as the top fabric. Starting from the centre, pin along the top edge, turning under 2 cm, as you pin. Pin along the lower edge, if it is shaped, snip on the curves to allow it to lie flat. Slipstitch the two layers of fabric together all round the edge **130.**

Along the complete length of the back of the pelmet, sew a length of 2 cm cotton webbing. The top edge of the tape should be level with the top edge of the pelmet and the stitching should be along the lower edge of the tape (or webbing). The stitch should be a back stitch, and should at intervals, be taken through the buckram, without of course going through to the front face of the pelmet **131.**

This tape is to be used to tack the pelmet to the wooden lath. Starting at the centre of both board and pelmet, tack with small upholstery tacks ($\frac{1}{2}$ inch fine) at intervals of approximately 15 cm. Pull the pelmet firmly towards outer edge of the board as you tack, this ensures that it stays flat. (If the pelmet is left slack it will buckle and ruin the buckram.)

### Trimming a pelmet

To make a pelmet more decorative, it can be trimmed with fringe or braid. There are many and varied ways of trimming. The usual way would be to sew a fringe on the lower edge. A matching braid can be added to the top edge but this does depend on the depth of the pelmet. Braids, can be used on the face of the pelmet to form patterns. This is particularly effective if both the curtains and pelmet are in plain fabric. A stab stitch should be used to attach the trimming. This stitch goes right through the buckram, and holds the trimming firmly in place **132.**

When trimming a curve, gather along the inside edge of the trimming to make it fit the curve **133**.

When turning a corner, mitre the trimming by folding; never cut any away **134**.

Valances are used in the same way as a pelmet, however they are made of material only and as they have no buckram they are easily washed. Many people prefer valances for bedroom windows as they give a softer effect than a pelmet. Variations can be made by making different types of headings (see *Curtain headings*, Chapter 4) **135**.

Measure the width required across the window including returns. For a gathered valance you must then double this measurement. For box pleats take two and half times the width. Measure the depth required and add 8 cm on each length for turnings. Cut the required number of lengths and seam them together. Cut and join the lining in the same way.

Pin the lining and fabric together, right sides facing. Stitch 2 cm seam along the *lower* edge **136**.

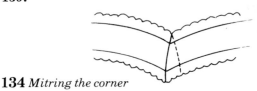

**134** *Mitring the corner*

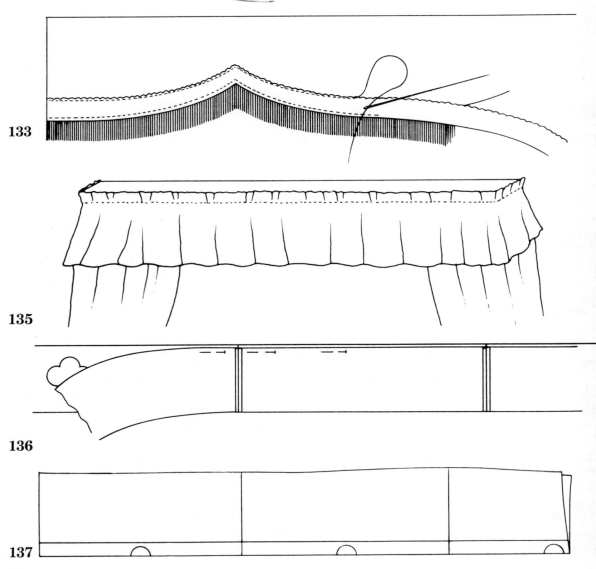

**133**

**135**

**136**

**137**

Press all seams open, fold the seam up until 2 cm of the fabric shows on the lining side. Fold both ends in and slipstitch **137**.

Measure the valance to the depth required. Finish the top, by heading with a pleating tape, in the same way as a curtain heading (see page 31) **138**.

If the valance is to be tacked on to a board, a loop of tape should be inserted every 15 cm along the length of the heading. The tacks can then be placed through the loops to avoid damage to the material **139**.

A valance rail may be used, and in this case, a flat hook is inserted in the heading tape, at intervals of $7\frac{1}{2}$ cm **140**.

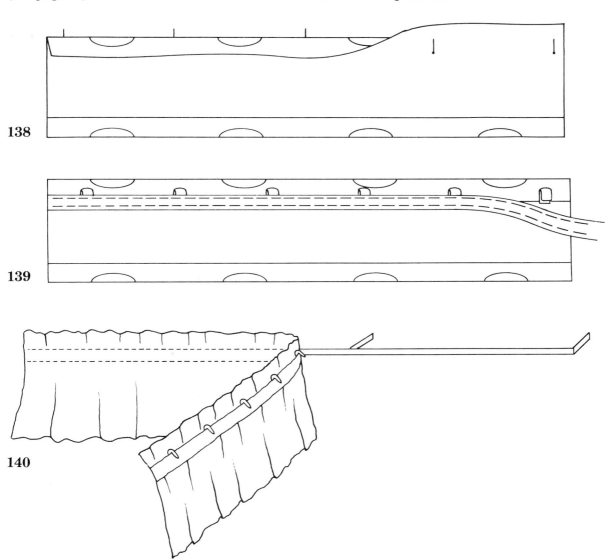

**138**

**139**

**140**

# Swags and tails

Swags and tails are used as a decorative pelmet, with or without curtains. To look really elegant, they need to be used at a high window or in a room with a high ceiling. The reason for this is that as swags need to be fairly deep to obtain a good drape, using them at a shallow window tends to look out of proportion and top heavy. The tails are used either at each end of the window, to balance the swags, or they can be used in a more elaborate manner in between the swags as well **141**.

There are several types of tail shapes, the swags are however basically the same shape, the variations being made on the depth or width.

The arrangement can be made to suit the size of the window. A general guide for depth, would be to make the deepest part of the swag approximately a quarter of the depth of the curtain. The tails would be just over a third of the curtain depth. This is only a guide as it is a matter of personal choice, if you are not sure how deep you would like the finished arrangement, make them up in lining and pin into position on the pelmet board. When adjustments have been made, use the lining for a pattern when cutting the main

*Making a 'mock-up' in lining*

fabric. The lining can be used to line the swags. The tails are lined with the main fabric or a contrasting fabric as when they turn back, the underside is turned to the front.

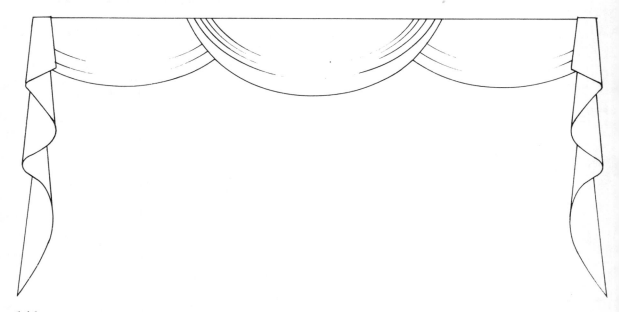

**141** *A simple arrangement of three swags and two jabot end tails*

## Cutting and making a basic swag

When cutting a swag allow at least double the finished depth required.

Cut the swag to the basic shape. Mark the pleat marks at intervals. These must be marked exactly the same both sides to make the finished folds even. The amount of pleats depend on the type of fabric used, generally it looks better to have deeper pleats, and not too many **142**.

**142**

Start folding from the bottom up to the top. When using a heavy fabric it is best to fold the swag first and line the finished shape afterwards. With a thin fabric the swag can be lined first, then pleated in one with the main fabric **143**.

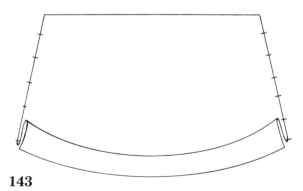

**143**

To line the swag before pleating, cut an identical shape in lining and place right sides together. Machine round the sides and lower edge, leaving all the top open. Turn right side out, and press. Now the swag can be pleated as above **144**.

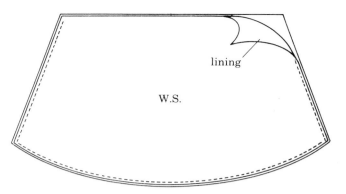

**144** *Lining the swag before pleating*

To line a swag after pleating, cut the lining to the *finished* size of the swag. Turn under the edges and slipstitch in place. The top can be slipstitched at this stage **145**.

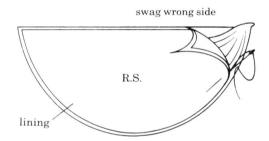

**145** *Lining the swag after pleating*

Place a tack tape, a length of cotton webbing is ideal, along the top edge of the swag, and sew in place. The swag is now ready to tack in place on the pelmet board **146**.

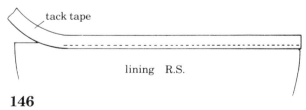

**146**

## Cutting and making a jabot tail

This type of tail can be used as a break between swags, as well as a finish on each end of the swag arrangement. To gain the best effect most tails are lined in a contrasting material, this shows the folds to the best advantage **147, 148.**

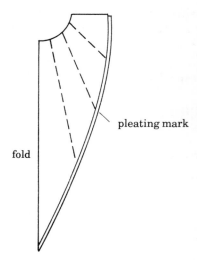

**150** *Shape for jabot centre tail (cut one on double fabric)*

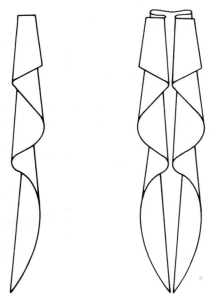

**147** *Jabot tail (end)*     **148** *Jabot tail (centre)*

To cut the tail, decide the depth required, keep the width in proportion, and allow for turnings **149, 150.**

Cut the lining in exactly the same way as the main material. Place lining and fabric, right sides together, and machine $1\frac{1}{2}$ cm in from the edge, leaving a small opening at the top. Turn right side out. Press carefully so that the edges make a clean line.

Turn the top over, neaten the edges, and sew on a tack tape, in the same manner as for the swags **151.**

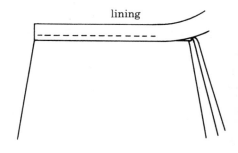

**151**

After tacking the swags in position on the pelmet board, place the tail at each end so that it just overlaps the last swag by approximately 8 cm, *not* right at the extreme of the upturn of the swag **152, 153**

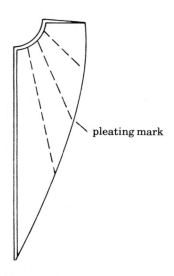

**149** *Shape for jabot end tails (cut the pair together)*

44

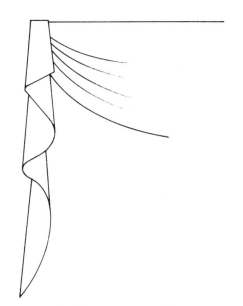

**152** *Swag and tail hanging correctly*

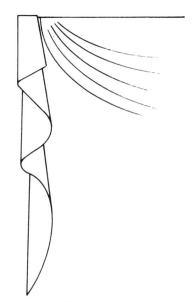

**153** *Swag and tail hanging incorrectly*

## Bell tail

This is used mainly between swags, and the lining is usually in a contrasting fabric **154**.

The cutting plan for the bell tail is as shown below. This is a basic shape, and can be varied according to individual taste. The main fabric is cut with the short side to the fold, and the lining is cut with the long side to the fold. The reason for this is that the seams are then hidden on the right side when the tail is hanging **155, 156**.

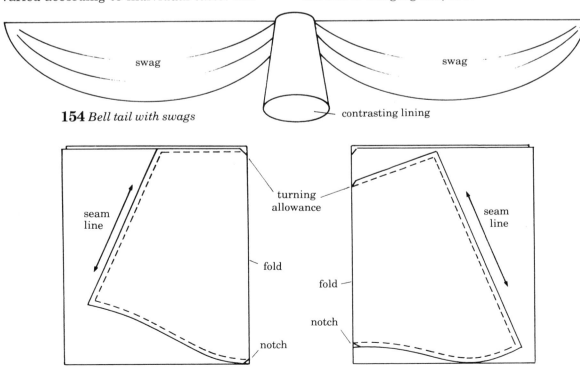

**154** *Bell tail with swags*

**155** *Cutting plan for lining*

**156** *Cutting plan for main fabric*

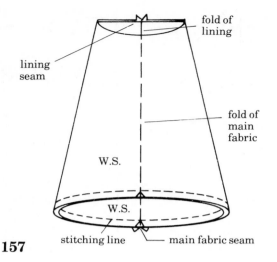

**157**

Mark the centre of each fold with a notch, this will make it easier to line up the two pieces of fabric when joining them.

Make up the bell tail by stitching each piece, the main fabric and the lining, separately along its seamline. Open the seams and press flat. Turn both pieces so that the right side is facing in on the main fabric and the wrong side in on the lining.

Place the lining section inside the fabric section matching the notches to the seams. Machine stitch the two sections together at the base **157**.

Turn right side out and press the base seam. Line up the top edges, neaten the top edge and apply tack tape **158**.

Tack the tails onto the pelmet board after fixing the swags in position.

### Pleated end tail

This is used to cover the two ends of the swag, the length and depth of pleats depending on the size of the area to be covered **159, 160**.

Cut the tails together, right sides of the fabric facing, to make sure that you have an exact pair.

Cut the tail so that you have enough fabric to return round the corner of the pelmet board. Mark the pleats on both tails. Cut the lining in the same manner as the main fabric **161**.

Lay the main fabric and lining right sides together, and machine round the sides and lower edge.

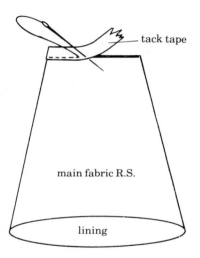

**158**

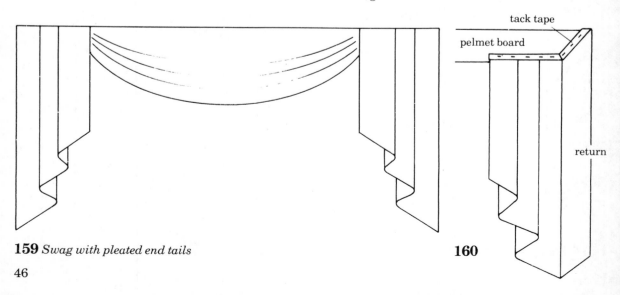

**159** *Swag with pleated end tails*

**160**

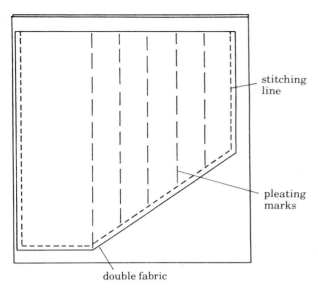

stitching line

pleating marks

double fabric

**161** *Cutting plan for pleated end tails*

Turn the right side out and press the edges all round. Pleat the fabric at the marks, concertina fashion **162, 163.**

Press in place and neaten the top edge. Attach the tack tape, and fix the tails at either end of the pelmet board.

If the tail is to be trimmed it should be done before it is pleated. The trimming is slipstitched in place through the front fabric only **164, 165.**

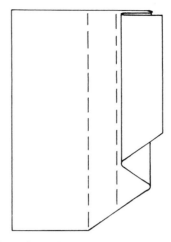

**163** *Folding the tail*

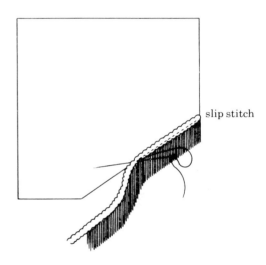

slip stitch

**164** *Trimming the end tail before pleating*

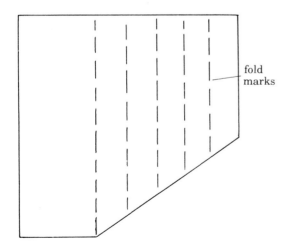

fold marks

**162** *End tail ready to be pleated*

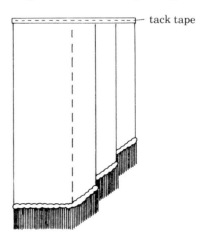

tack tape

**165** *The end tail ready to hang*

# 9: Net curtains

Net curtains, or glass curtains as they are sometimes called, are made from transparent fabric. Several types of fabrics are suitable including Terylene, nylon, Tergal and voile. The disadvantage of net curtaining is that it does tend to block out some of the light. The advantages, however, tend to outweigh the disadvantages. The effect of a net is to soften the hard outline of a window, also it affords privacy without blocking out the view. Many styles of ready-made nets are now sold, and as they are available in most window sizes, with only the side hems needing to be sewn to make them fit, they have become very popular. However, not every window is a standard size, and if a plain or special style is required they must be cut and made individually.

## Plain nets

To make a plain net curtain the method of cutting and sewing is the same method used in making unlined curtains (see Chapter 5). The heading tape used, however, should be made of nylon or Tervoil. If the nets are to be hung from an expanding wire or a rod, then a heading and a slot must be made at the top **166.**

## Drape nets

This treatment is most effective on a large wide window, it tends to clutter either a small or a tall window **167, 168.**

The nets are usually frilled at the edges, either on both sides (see diagram) or they can be frilled at the draped edge only. The top is made with a heading and a slot. It is not

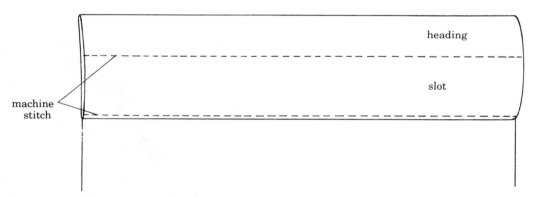

**166** *Slot heading*

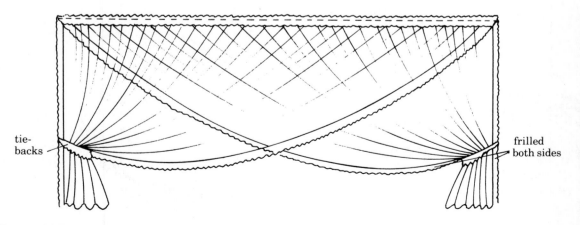

**167** *Full drape nets (fitted on two separate rods or wires)*

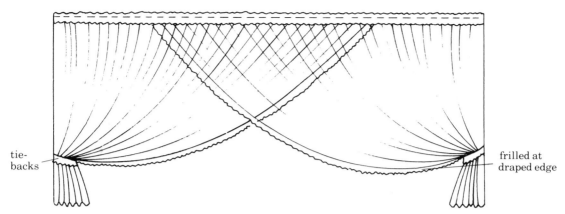

**168** *Half drape nets (fitted on two separate rods or wires)*

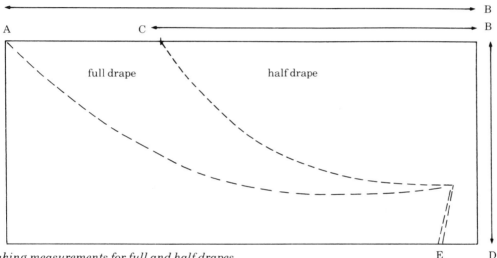

**169** *Taking measurements for full and half drapes*

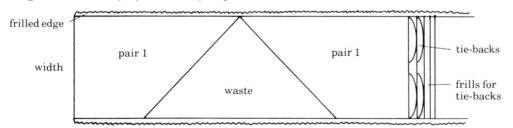

**170** *Cutting plan for one pair of drapes on ready frilled fabric*

necessary to use tape and hooks on these nets, as once they are arranged in folds they are not moved. The drapes are held back in position by *tie-backs*, shaped bands which can be frilled or plain (see below).

To estimate the amount of fabric needed, measure the window area. For a full drape allow double fullness (of the window width) and for a half drape, allow one and a half times fullness. For the length measurement, take the measurement from A to E (following the dotted line in diagram **169**), for full drape, or C to E for half drape. Take depth of window B to D. Allow 20 cm extra on these measurements for hems and headings **169**.

To cut the fabric, plan as economically as possible. As the drapes have to be paired, it is more economical to cut two pairs at once **170, 171.**

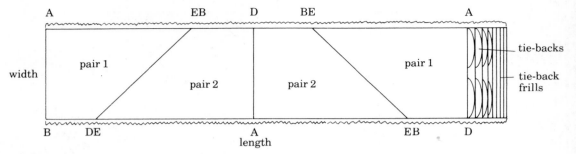

**171** *Cutting plan for two pairs of drapes on ready frilled fabric*

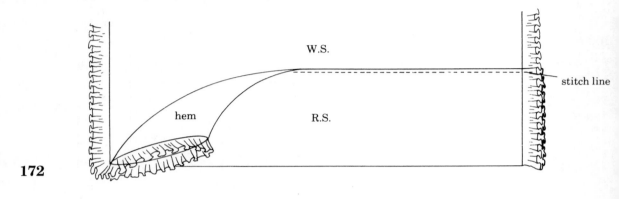

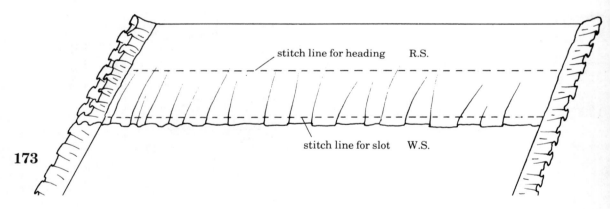

After cutting the drapes to size, if you are adding your own frills do so at this stage. Fold the bottom edge (D to E) up 4 cm then 4 cm again, making a double hem. Machine the hem along the edge. Ease the fullness in as you sew (the fullness is caused by the cross grain of fabric) **172.**

Measure the length B to D to fit the window size, and turn over the top edge 6 cm, then 6 cm again. Machine along the edge as previously done on the bottom hem. Finish the ends very securely. Measure 3 cm from the top edge of the curtain all along the length of the curtain, marking a line. Machine along the marked line, this then divides the heading from the slot **173.**

Before hanging the drape nets, the tie-backs must be made. These are shaped bands that are to hold the nets in position after they have been draped. The approximate length is about 45 cm, depending on the volume of net to be held. Each tie-back must be cut double with a turning of 1½ cm allowed. A 5 cm length of tape for each end of the tie-back, should be cut at this stage. With the right sides together, stitch as shown in diagram

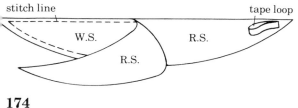

stitch line

W.S.

R.S.

R.S.

tape loop

**174**

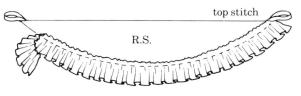

top stitch

R.S.

**175**

inserting the folded tapes at each corner, to form a loop, and leaving a gap to turn the tie-back right side out **174**.

Turn right side out and close gap with slipstitching. If the tie-back is to be trimmed with a frill, top stitch this along the shaped edge **175**.

Press the tie-backs and the drape nets. Thread the rod or wire through the slot at the top of the drapes **176**.

After threading the rod through the net, gather it up by pushing into small folds, keep these even all along the rod. Fit one rod behind the other, under the soffit, with the wrong side facing out to the road. Starting with the long side of the drape, fold up keeping the same distance from the bottom edge, all the way along **177**.

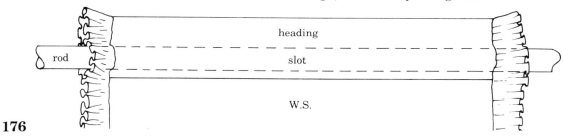

heading

rod

slot

W.S.

**176**

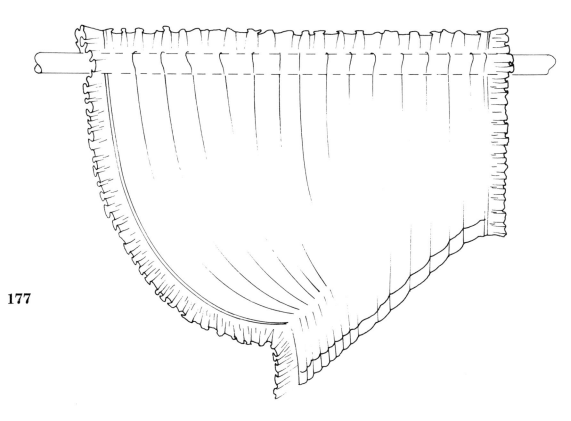

**177**

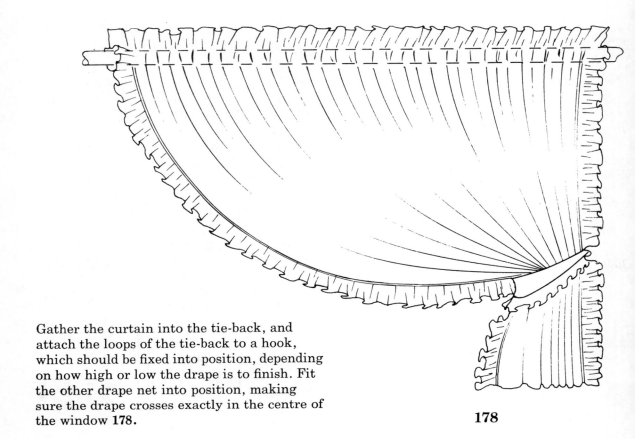

Gather the curtain into the tie-back, and
attach the loops of the tie-back to a hook,
which should be fixed into position, depending
on how high or low the drape is to finish. Fit
the other drape net into position, making
sure the drape crosses exactly in the centre of
the window 178.

178

# Festoon nets

Festoon nets are very elaborate to look at, but fairly simple to make. They do tend to block out the light, although they are sheer, because of the many folds in them. To measure for festoons you will require one and a half times the width of the window, and three times the length. Decide on the width of the festoon (average size is approximately 30 cm) and mark the fabric in parallel lines on the wrong side (mark with tailors chalk or, if preferred, a line of tacking stitches **179**.

After marking in the festoons, turn the side edge in until the raw edge is level with the outer festoon line. Press down and tack in place. Using 1½ cm Terylene tape, place it on the marked lines, with the centre of the tape exactly on the centre of each line. Pin in position and machine down the outer edges of the tape **180**.

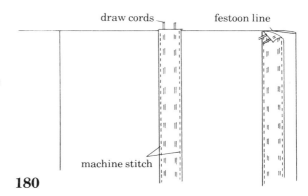

**180**

Leave the ends at the top and bottom of the net raw. Turn the hem at the lower edge up 2 cm and press in place. Turn the raw edge under 1 cm and machine along this line, catching in all the cords on the way. Make certain the cords are caught by double stitching over each of them **181**.

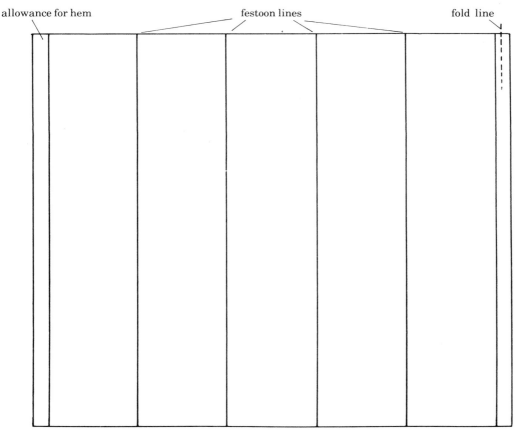

**179** *Marking plan for festoon nets*

The top can be finished with either a slot
heading or a gathered heading using
standard tape in white nylon (see Chapter 7).
Pull up the heading to the required length
and make a cleat at the end. Pull up each
festoon to fit the window size. The finished
measurement should be taken from the base
of the scallop, not from the base of the tape
**182**.

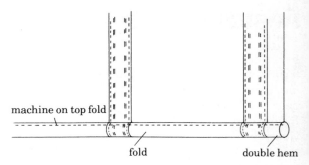

machine on top fold

fold

double hem

**181**

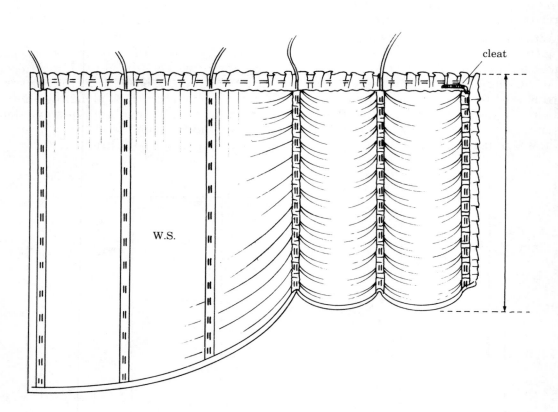

cleat

W.S.

**182**

After pulling up all the tapes to the correct size, make a cleat with the ends and stitch the cleats neatly along the top of the heading tape. Using a long loose machine stitch, or by hand, stitch a line right down the centre of each length of tape. This will hold the gathers in place. This is necessary because the weight of the gathers will gradually drop towards the bottom and make the gathering uneven.

Place nylon hooks in the heading and hang in place **183**.

If a slot heading is used thread the rod or wire through the slot and even out the gathers starting in the centre and working towards the outer edges. A variation of the festoon can be made by adding a frill at the bottom edge, this must be added at the hemming stage (see diagram) **184**.

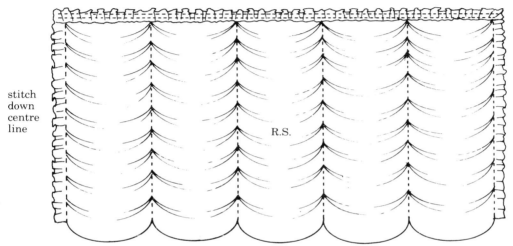

stitch down centre line

R.S.

**183** *Festoon with gathered heading tape*

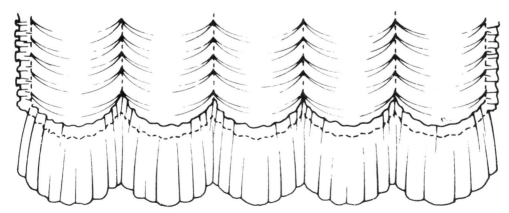

**184** *Festoon with frilled base*

# 10: Roller blinds

For certain windows—kitchens and bathrooms for example—roller blinds are more suitable than curtains. They are also good for tiny windows, perhaps in an old cottage, or for dormer windows in a bedroom, as they are completely out of the way during the day time.

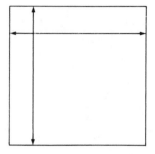

**185** *Fitted into recess*

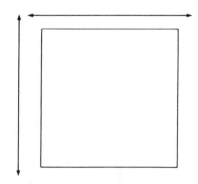

**186** *Fitted outside recess*

There is a very good range of roller blinds available, both ready-made and made-to-measure. If, however, the fabric required is not in the range it is expensive to have a length of fabric laminated for one blind. A perfectly good blind can be made from a length of fabric, using a spray made for the purpose of stiffening blinds. A kit for making blinds can be bought from department or DIY stores. This consists of: one wooden roller, with an internal spring fitted in one end, one wooden lath for the base, one pair of brackets and screws, fixing plate, cord and acorn, 4 mm tacks (or staples may be used). To complete, the materials required are: one can of spray stiffener, length of fabric, thread to match fabric, fringe or braid (optional). To measure the size of roller required, take the measurements as shown in diagrams.

It is a matter of choice whether the blind fits into the window recess or just outside it **185, 186.**

If fitting inside the recess, the measurements must be taken with a firm rule not a tape measure. The fabric will not fit right to the edges of the recess as an allowance has to be made for the brackets. The blind will be finished 4 cm less than the recess measurement. The roller may not be available in the exact size needed so the nearest larger size should be purchased. To cut the roller to size, measure along the roller including the pin at either end. The *pin width* (length of

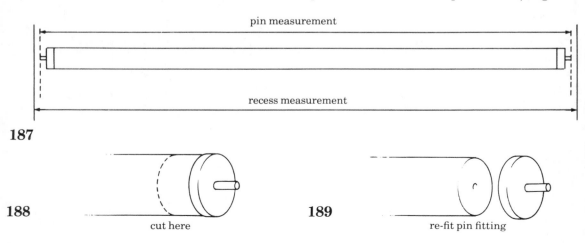

pin measurement

recess measurement

**187**

**188**

cut here

**189**

re-fit pin fitting

roller plus both pins) should be $\frac{1}{2}$ cm less than the recess measurement (to allow for the brackets) **187**.

Remove the end of the roller, opposite the spring-loaded end and cut the wood to size **188, 189**.

Replace the fitting and hammer in place. Cut the length of fabric, at least 30 cm wider than the required width and 40 cm longer than the required length. At this stage make a seam in the fabric if it is not wide enough, the seam must be a lapped seam and the amount of fabric to be added should be equal each side of the centre width.

The fabric should then be hung up and sprayed carefully, taking care not to miss any areas. If possible the spray should be used out of doors, or in the bathroom with the windows open. Spray both sides of the fabric and allow to dry completely. When the fabric is dry it will stiffen. Lay the fabric flat on a table, and measure the length, this is

necessary because it may have shrunk during the spraying process. The length must now be cut square. This is most important as otherwise the blind will not run smoothly. Measure the width across the roller and deduct $1\frac{1}{2}$ cm. This is the *finished* size. Add 8 cm. This allows for turnings of 4 cm at each side. This is the *cut* size. Cut the width to size, making sure it is square. Turn in the sides 4 cm and using a zigzag stitch sew down the side turnings. Turn up the bottom turning and machine across. (The lath should be cut $2\frac{1}{2}$ cm shorter than the finished blind size). Machine down one side of hem and insert lath. Machine other end of the hem enclosing lath **190**.

Having placed the lath in the hem, measure the centre point along the lath and fit the cord and fixing plate in place, and thread cord through the acorn. Knot the cord and cut off the ends **191**.

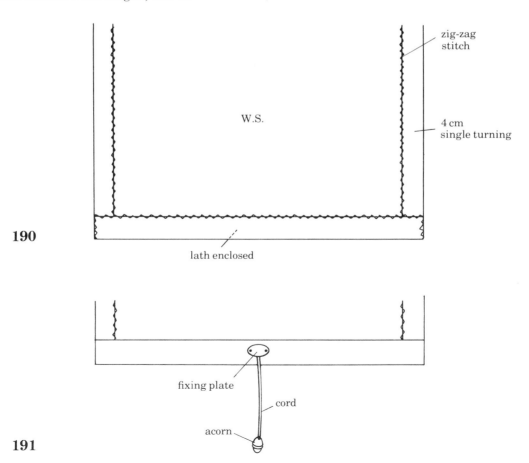

zig-zag stitch

4 cm single turning

W.S.

**190**

lath enclosed

fixing plate

cord

acorn

**191**

Leave the cord long enough to be able to pull the blind down without having to stretch up for it. After finishing the bottom of the blind, the top must now be tacked to the roller. The roller has a line already marked across between the pins. The blind must be tacked exactly in place on this line, the right side of the blind should be tacked to the roller. The spring-loaded end will be to the left of the blind **192, 193**.

Once the top has been tacked to the roller, roll the fabric round the roller keeping the sides level **194**.

The right and left bracket are slightly different. The left one has a cut-out and a centre hole, the right one has a centre hole only. Place the brackets in position, and mark the screw holes with a pencil, make a hole with a bradawl on these marks, place the screws in and screw right home **195, 196**.

Place the blind in the brackets, with the blind rolled up. Pull the blind down, and take it out of the brackets. Roll the blind up again by hand and replace in the brackets. This

**195** *Left hand bracket*   **196** *Right hand bracket*

loads the spring in the roller. If the blind does not rewind now, repeat the process until the blind rolls up easily. To stop the blind, in any position, pull slightly forward and let it click into place. Give a slight downward pull to release the blind and it will re-roll automatically.

### Blind finishes
Instead of a plain finish at the bottom, several forms of decoration can be added. Braid can be glued on to the stitched edge above the lath, or a fringe can be glued at the lower edge **197, 198.**

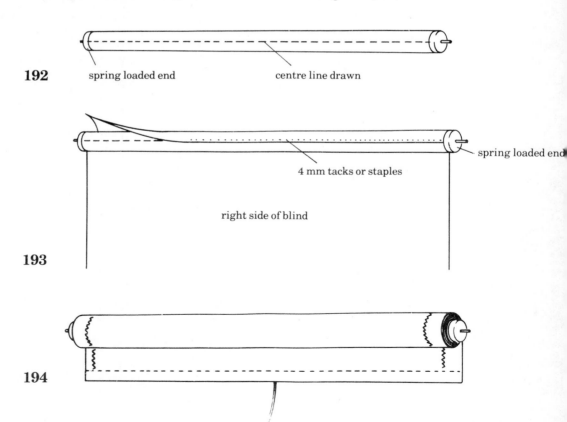

**192**    spring loaded end          centre line drawn

spring loaded end

4 mm tacks or staples

right side of blind

**193**

**194**

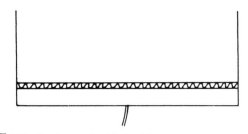

**197** *Blind trimmed with braid*

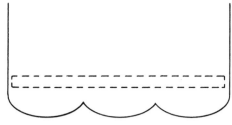

**199** *Shaped blind, right side*

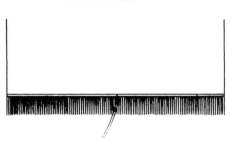

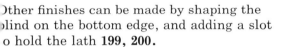

**198** *Blind trimmed with a fringe*

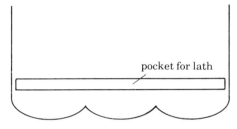

**200** *Shaped blind, wrong side*

Other finishes can be made by shaping the blind on the bottom edge, and adding a slot to hold the lath **199, 200.**

To make the slot for the lath, a strip of the fabric 7 cm deep and the same size as the finished width of the blind should be attached. Do not cut the shape required until the blind has been stiffened and cut square, and the side hems turned in and machined.

Mark the centre at the bottom edge and start the design from here. Work out the design on a length of paper, before transferring it to the blind **201, 202.**

Cut out the design, and place the centre to the halfway mark. Draw round the design and repeat again at quarter marks, until the design is complete **203, 204.**

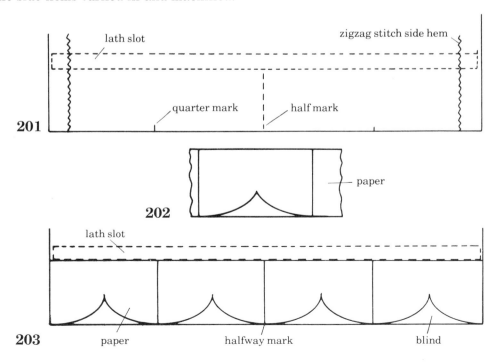

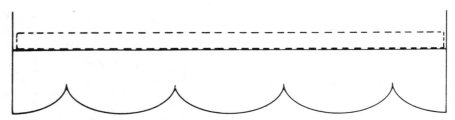

**204** *Excess blind material cut away*

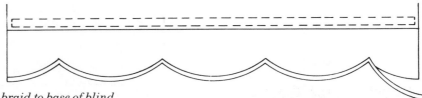

**205** *Attaching braid to base of blind*

Outline the bottom edge of the blind with fringe or braid. This can be stitched in place with zigzag stitch or it can be glued with a fabric glue **205**.

A selection of designs for the base of blinds. These can be varied to suit the width, extend or compress the design as necessary **206, 207, 208, 209, 210, 211.**

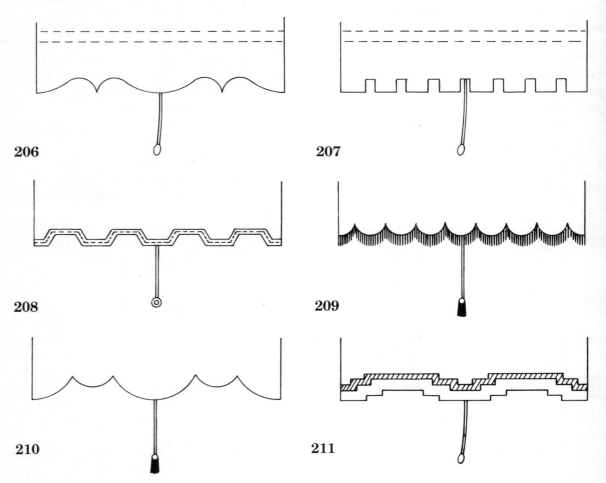

**206**

**207**

**208**

**209**

**210**

**211**

# 11: Piping and ruching

## Cutting and making piping

This method of trimming is used on loose covers, cushions and upholstery. Most upholsterers call it welting, loose cover makers call it piping and most dress makers call it a crossway strip. It is one and the same thing.

To cut piping place the length of fabric on the table, and taking the corner between the fingers, fold over towards opposite side, making a right angle **212**.

Cut along the fold, and measure from the cut edge, strips of 3½ cm. Cut into lengths 25 cm of 122 cm width fabric makes 6.50 m of piping **213**.

Join piping across diagonally (this will be on

*Cutting crossway strips of fabric for piping*

the straight grain of fabric) with right sides together **214**.

Trim the turnings to 1½ cm and open out flat **215**.

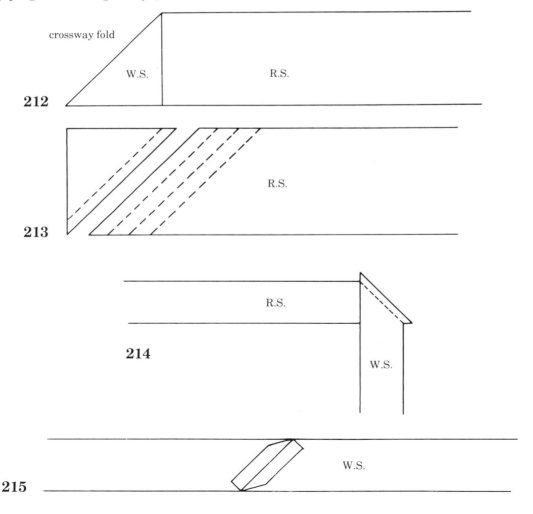

Lay pre-shrunk piping cord, in the centre of the prepared length of piping, and fold over lengthwise. Using a piping or zip foot, machine stitch along the length keeping the foot close to the cord but without catching it in the stitching. The piping is now ready for use **216.**

Piping cord is made in different gauges, for a thick fabric choose a thin cord, and vice-versa. If the cord is not pre-shrunk, boil it before use, this prevents it shrinking after it is made up, thus making the piping wrinkle.

To pipe a cushion or similar article, the piping has to be joined when the two ends meet.

Join the ends diagonally (on the straight grain of the fabric) and trim away the excess turnings, making sure the piping fits the piece of fabric to be piped **217.**

To complete the join, lay the two pieces of cord side by side, and cut directly through the centre **218.**

The cord should now butt together without leaving any gap **219.**

Place the cord back into the centre of the piping, fold over, and continue the line of stitching **220.**

Another method of joining the cord is by splicing it, as shown in the following diagram **221.**

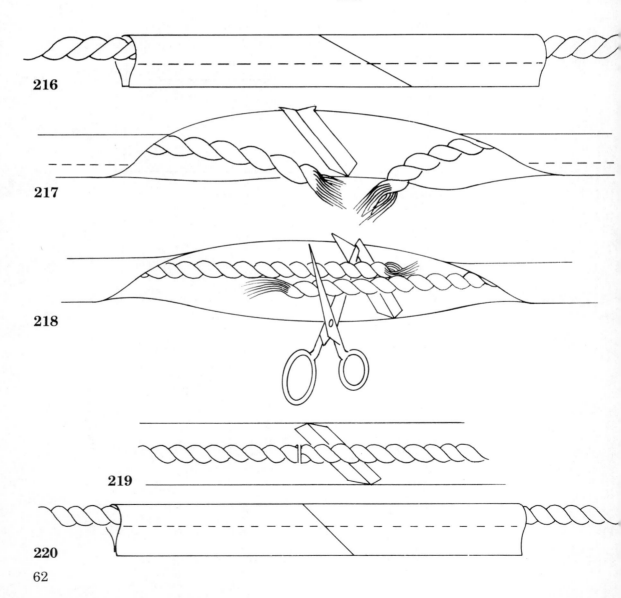

216

217

218

219

220

62

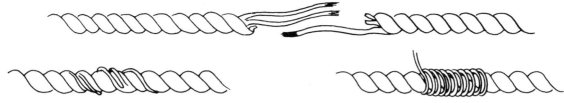

**221**

# Cutting and making ruching

### Gathered ruching

This trimming can be used on cushions, bedcovers and eiderdowns. You will need more fabric to make it than piping but it gives a more elaborate finish.

Cut strips of fabric $7\frac{1}{2}$ cm wide across the width of the fabric (three strips of 122 cm width fabric, will make enough ruching for a cushion 50 cm square).

Join strips together to make one long strip. Place pre-shrunk cord in the centre and fold over lengthwise **222.**

Make a pleat, every $1\frac{1}{2}$ cm by folding fabric under, or using the gathering foot on the machine. Gather along the length by machining $\frac{1}{2}$ cm from the edge. Do not catch the piping cord on the stitching. This should be pushed into the centre well away from the stitching at this stage **223.**

Join the ends of the ruching (this completes the circle). Pull the cord until it is the right size for the cushion cover or article which is being ruched. If the cord is left slack inside the ruche, it will not pleat evenly **224.**

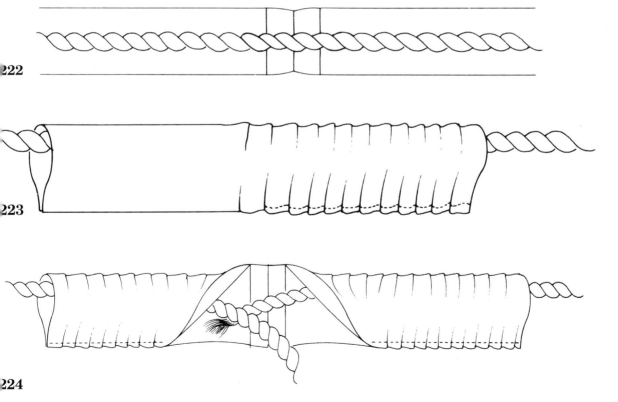

**222**

**223**

**224**

Splice the cord as shown in diagram **221.**

Pleat remaining ruching, so that the join is not visible. Attach ruching to the cushion cover **225, 226.**

When turning a corner with the ruching make sure it is extra full at the actual corner this enables the ruche to be pulled square on the finished cushion **227.**

seam

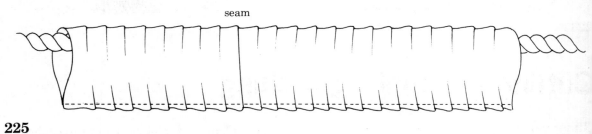

**225**

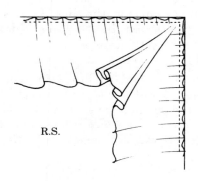

R.S.

**226** *Applying the ruching*

**227** *The finished corner*

# 12: Cushions and bolsters

Cushions and bolsters are not only comfortable, but can add an eye-catching and individual look to a room.

## Flat cushion covers

Measure the size of the finished cushion cover required. Add turnings each side of $1\frac{1}{2}$ cm.

If the cushion is not more than half a width of fabric, cut as shown in diagram.
Make sure, if the fabric is patterned, that the

pattern is in the centre of the cushion **228**.

If the cushion takes over the half width, use the centre of the fabric if it is patterned, or place close to one side if it is plain. The spare pieces are used for piping **229, 230**.

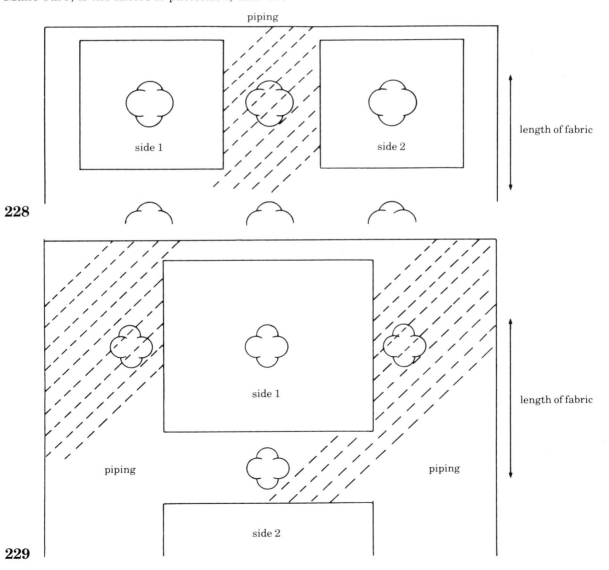

**228**

**229**

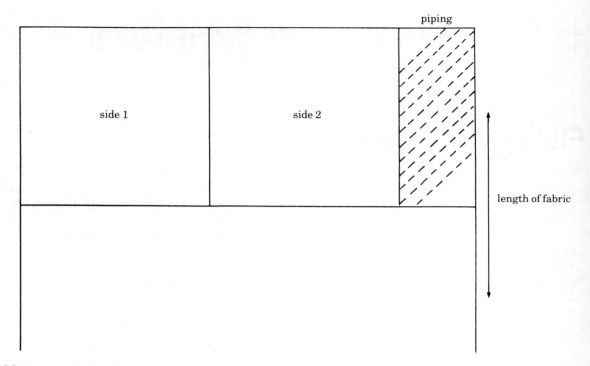

**230** *Cutting plan for plain fabric*

Lay the fabric out flat. Cut the top edge of fabric to the thread so that it is square to the selvedge. Cut out the cushion pieces, and the strips of piping.

Join and make up a length of piping. (See *Piping* Chapter 11)

Starting in the middle of the bottom edge, place the piping along the edge (raw edge of piping to raw edge of cushion) and pin in position. Always pipe the top side of the cushion so that the zip is hidden.

Stitch the piping in position. When the machine needle is at the corner, leave the needle in the fabric, lift the presser foot,

slash the piping right to the corner, turn, replace the presser foot and continue stitching **231.**

Complete stitching, until the two ends are within 10 cm. Join the ends of the piping (see *Piping* Chapter 11). Finish the stitching.

At this stage the zip can be inserted with ease. The zip should be long enough to reach within 5 cm of each end of the bottom edge of the cushion.

Lay the piped side of the cushion, face down onto the underneath side of the cushion, right sides facing **232.**

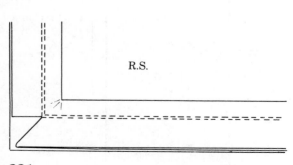

**231**

**232**

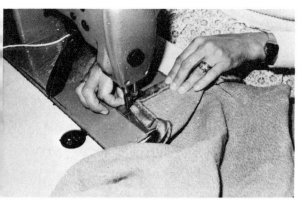

*Piping the corner of a flat cushion cover*

Stitch the two pieces together, along the seam line for 5 cm from each outside edge **233**.

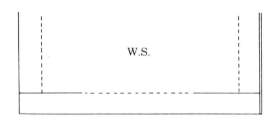

**233**

Open the cushion so that it lies flat. Place the zip underneath the opening, and tack into position. Machine all round the zip keeping as close as possible to the teeth **234**.

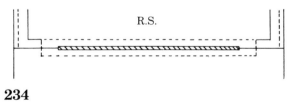

**234**

Close cushion, so that right sides are together. Pin the remaining three sides

together, and keeping as close to the piping as possible, machine in position **235**.

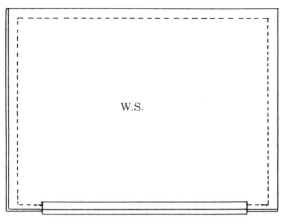

**235**

Trim edges and oversew to neaten or make another row of stitching close to the edge of the fabric. This will stop the edges from fraying.

Turn right side out and press. Insert filled pad and push well into the corners. (The inside pad should be 2 cm larger than the cushion cover to enable it to fill out correctly **236**.

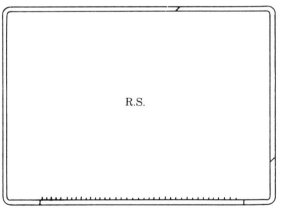

**236**

# Bordered cushions

A bordered cushion can be made to fit the contours of the chair. Cut the top and underside of the cushion in the same manner as the flat cushion, see page 65. Measure the borders and add 1½ cm each side for turnings. On the back border the seam allowance should be 3 cm each side, this is to allow for the zip to be inserted at the back. After cutting out, divide the back border in two, lengthwise **237**.

Cut the borders to the correct size, by pinning them to the cushion and fitting to the exact size. If patterned, make sure the pattern runs in line **238**.

Unpin the borders from the cushion and seam the sides and front in one length **239**. Place the two back border pieces together, right sides facing and stitch 5 cm from each end, leaving the centre open. Neaten both ends **240**.

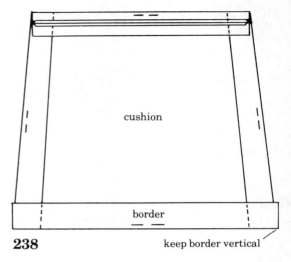

cushion

border

**238**

keep border vertical

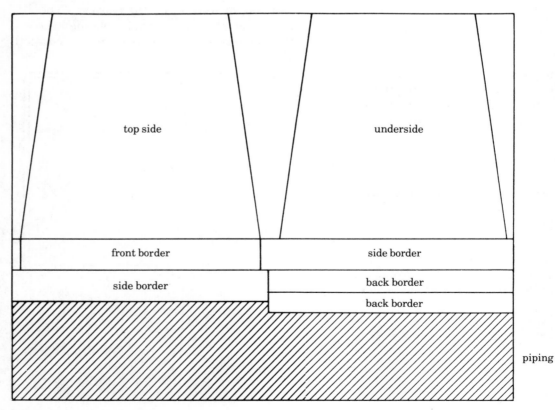

top side

underside

front border

side border

side border

back border

back border

piping

**237** *Cutting plan for a bordered cushion*

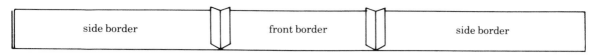

side border        front border        side border

**239**

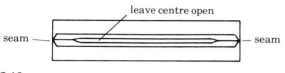

leave centre open

seam — — seam

**240**

Place the zip underneath the opening and pin into position. Make sure the zip is completely concealed. Sew with a zipper foot, as close to the teeth of the zip as possible **241.**

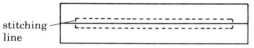

stitching line

**241**

Stitch the back border on to the two side borders, thus completing the square **242.**

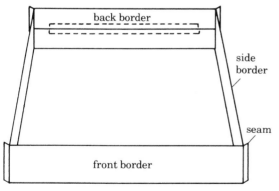

back border

side border

seam

front border

**242**

Neaten the seams before going onto the next stage. Starting at the back border, pipe the border all round, joining where the two ends meet at the back. (See *Cutting and making piping* Chapter 11). Pipe the other side of the border, making the join at the back **243.**

Assemble the cushion by placing the top of the border to the cushion top, lining up the pattern and matching up the corners. To enable the piping to go smoothly round the corners snip into the corners at an angle to allow the fabric to spread **244.**

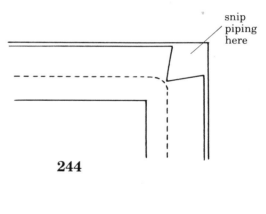

snip piping here

**244**

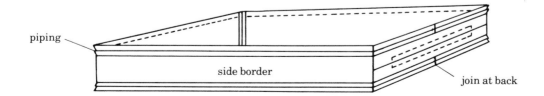

piping

side border

join at back

**243**

When the corners are in position, machine in place keeping close to the cord to give a good even line. After machining the cushion top, repeat with the base of the cushion. Neaten the seams, and turn right side out. Press and fit on to the cushion. To ease the cushion pad into the cover, fold it in half lengthways, and push the front of the pad into the opening. Push right into the front corners, before releasing the cushion and allowing it to fill out the rest of the cover **245.**

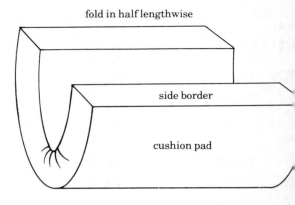

**245**

# Making a bolster cover

This type of cushion makes a practical, as well as decorative, back support. A divan can be converted into a seating area with the use of three bolsters, particularly useful in a bed sitting room. Two bolsters of approximately 90 cm with end circles of 20 cm diameter make the ideal size for a divan **246.**

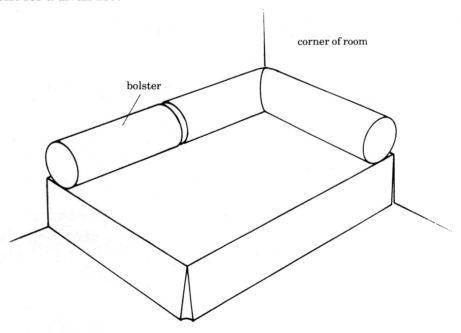

**246** *Kick pleat style divan cover*

To cut the bolster, first lay your fabric out
flat on the table, and square it up. Mark out
across the width of the fabric the
measurement required then add 3 cm, this
will give you 1½ cm turning at either end **247**.

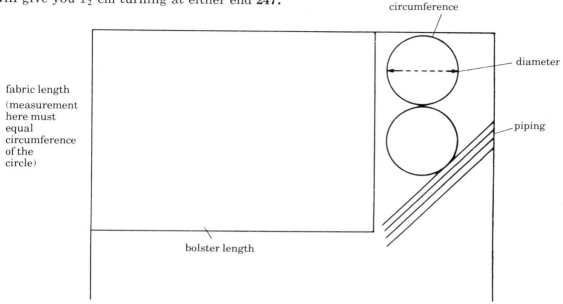

fabric length
(measurement
here must
equal
circumference
of the
circle)

circumference

diameter

piping

bolster length

**247** *Cutting plan for bolster*

Having cut out the bolster, the next step is to
pin the end circles in place. To make sure
that these are placed in parallel positions
eventually, they are now placed face to face.
The main fabric is folded across its length so
that the right sides are facing **248**.

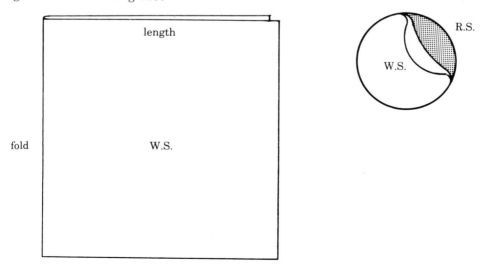

length

fold

W.S.

R.S.

W.S.

**248**

Proceed to pin the end circles onto the end sections, at this stage both pieces will be double thickness of fabric. If the fabric is patterned, the base of the pattern on the end circle should line up with the seam on the bolster **249**.

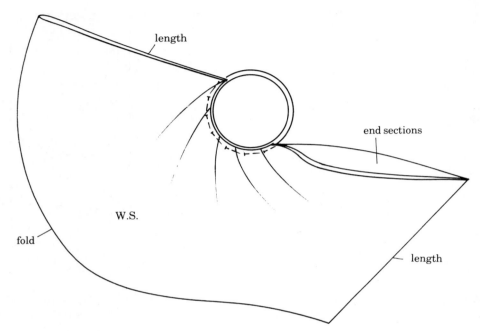

**249**

Continue to pin together until the two long sides meet. Pin these along the length from the circle to the fold. The bolster must now have notches cut at intervals around the circle and along the long seam. These act as markers when the bolster is assembled, to prevent the ends becoming twisted **250**.

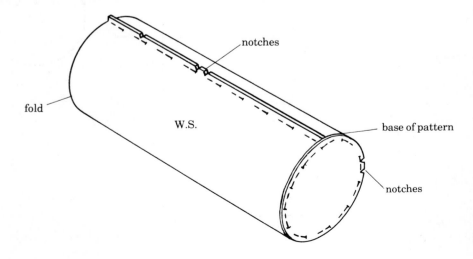

**250**

Assembling the bolster. Unpin the complete bolster and unfold the length. At this stage if a zip is to be used it should be inserted now (see bordered cushion). The zip is inserted in the long seam of the bolster, so that it lies underneath **251**.

After inserting the zip, unzip it for a short distance, this will enable you to turn the bolster right side out at a later stage. Join the piping in a length (see *Piping* Chapter 11) and pipe round the two end circles, joining the piping at the base, that is where the long seam will meet the end circles **252, 253**.

Placing the right sides together, pin the piped circles into either end of the bolster, matching the notches to ensure a good fit. Machine in place, and neaten the edges of the seams **254**.

*Piping the end circle of a bolster*

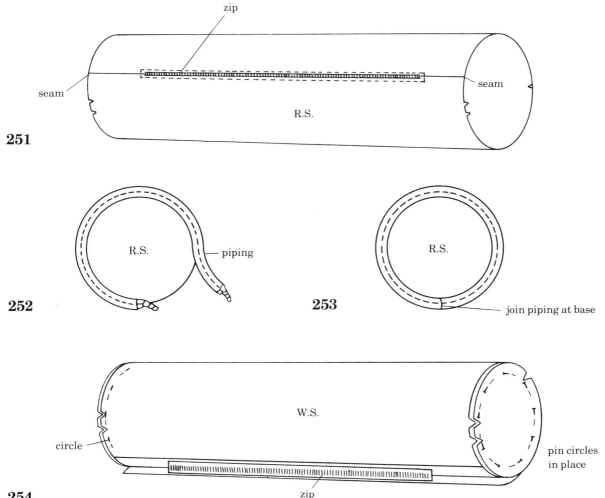

Turn the cover inside out and press **255**.

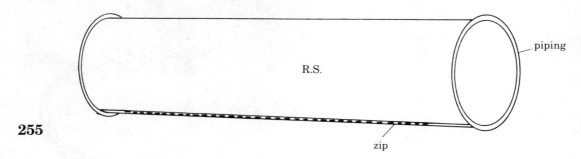

R.S.

piping

**255**

zip

To make the inside case, cut and assemble in exactly the same manner as the outer case, but omit the piping and the zip. If the case is to be filled with feather or down, it must be made of downproof cambric. If, however, the filling is foam chippings, sateen can be used. Make up the inside case and fill it with the type of filling required. Close the opening with a small slipstitch.

To fit the completed bolster into the outer case, fold it in half across the length and push both ends into the opening. Gradually push the ends of the bolster into the ends of the cushion, until the middle hump disappears. Never try to push one end completely in before the other or you may tear the zip **256**.

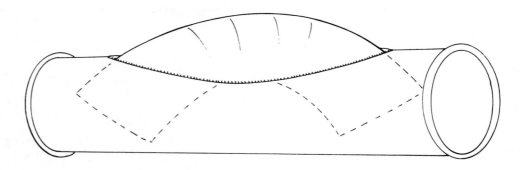

**256**

# 13: Loose covers for an easy chair

Making loose covers may seem a rather daunting prospect to the beginner, but it need not be if you tackle it in the right way.

## Estimating and cutting

**Estimating for a loose cover** (Chair with bordered seat cushion) When estimating a chair it is good practice to make out a *cut sheet*. This helps in cutting, as well as estimating, the fabric required. I have taken a basic chair shape. The same principles apply when measuring the settee, or other styles of chair. Make a list of the parts of the chair **257**.

Take the measurement of each piece, length first. Check on the list that you have allowed for two arms, as it is a common mistake to measure only one. On all the inside pieces allow an extra 15 cm for the tuck-in (see diagram **259**). The tuck-in is very important as it helps to hold the cover in place, so allow the fabric to tuck in wherever the chair requires it. When cutting a patterned fabric,

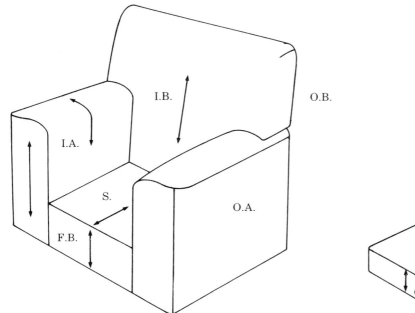

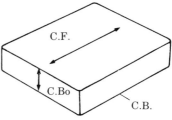

Arrow indicates length measurement

| | | | |
|---|---|---|---|
| I.B. | = Inside back | C.F. | = Cushion front |
| S. | = Seat | C.B. | = Cushion back |
| I.A. | = Inside arm | C.Bo. | = Cushion border |
| F.B. | = Front border | | |
| O.B. | = Outside back | | |

**257**

it is necessary to make all the patterns run in line. This gives the cover a professional finish, and is well worth the extra time involved **258**.

Make a 1½ cm allowance on all pieces for seaming. Transfer the measurements to the cut sheet **259, 260, 261**.

When estimating for a three piece suite, or more than one item, try to use all the spare pieces, without cutting into extra length. When the fabric is not wide enough for a particular piece, always join equal widths

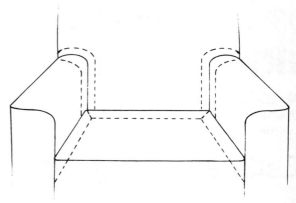

**259** *Loose cover showing the tuck-in area, denoted by dotted line*

either side of a centre length. Decide at this stage what base finish is required, and add the amount needed to the cut sheet. For a guide to the correct amount see *Base Finishes* below.

For a settee it is normally necessary to piece the fabric to get the required width for the larger sections, the inside back, outside back, seat and front border. This must be done in order to keep the pattern upright. A few fabrics however, can be used with the straight grain going across the chair, for example a plain or weave fabric. A pile fabric, even though it is plain must run with the pile going down.

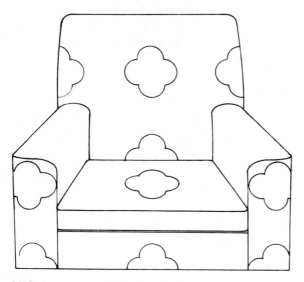

**258** *Pattern centralised on loose cover*

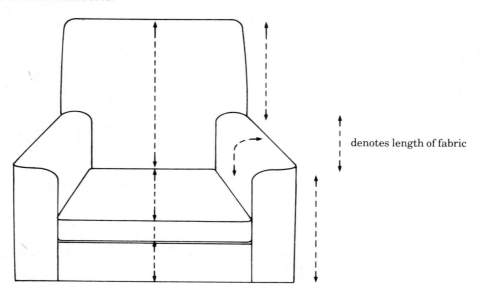

denotes length of fabric

**260** *Loose cover showing the direction in which all pieces of fabric must run*

| | Length cm | Width cm | | Length cm |
|---|---|---|---|---|
| | | | Fabric width 122 cm | |
| I.B. | 75 | 75 | I.B. | 75 |
| S. | 86 | 80 | S. | 86 |
| I.A. | 70 | 95 | I.A. | 70 |
| I.A. | 70 | 95 | I.A. | 70 |
| O.A. | 90 | 110 | O.A. | 90 |
| O.A. | 90 | 110 | O.A. | 90 |
| F.B. | 33 | 50 | F.B. | 33 |
| O.B. | 90 | 75 | O.B. | 90 |
| C.F. | 55 | 50 | C.F. | 55 |
| C.B. | 55 | 50 | C.B. | 15 |
| C.Bo | 15 | 105 | C.Bo | 15 |
| C.Bo | 15 | 105 | C.Bo | 15 |
| P. | 75 plus pieces | | Piping | 75 |

Add the lengths together 7.64 metres

**261** *Example of a cut sheet*

**Base finishes** There are several ways of finishing the base of a loose cover. For a tie-under style, add 15 cm to the length of all outside pieces. This allows for the fabric to be fitted underneath the chair and tied in place. For the kick pleat style, add four widths of fabric for a chair, and six for a small settee. Each width should be cut to a length of 20 cm depending on the depth of pleat required (20 cm gives a finished length of 15 cm). For a box pleated style you will need double the width of the measurement all round the base of the chair, an average chair takes five widths of fabric, and a settee takes eight widths. Each width should be cut to a length of 20 cm to give a finished length of 15 cm **262, 263, 264.**

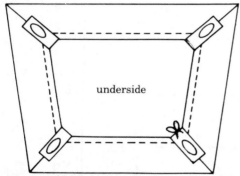

**262** *Tie-under finish, use on a tailored style loose cover*

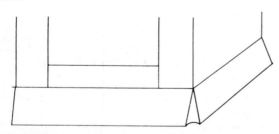

**263** *Kick pleat finish, for best effect use on a square type base*

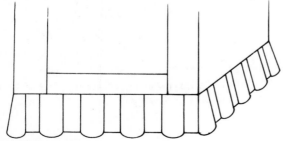

**264** *Box pleat finish, use on many styles of chair, particularly those with high legs*

# Cutting and pinning

Cut off lengths of cover as worked out on the cut sheet. Cut to the thread so that the fabric remains square, if however the fabric is patterned, keep to the pattern running across it even if it is not absolutely on the thread. (Many printed fabrics are not printed completely to a straight thread). Mark all the pieces on the wrong side with tailor's chalk. Mark with abbreviations for example (I.B. Chair) (I.A. Ch).

Both inside and outside arms must be paired, that is, insides match each other, outsides match each other. After cutting and marking all the pieces, prepare the chair for cutting the cover to shape. The chair is usually cut 'on the half'. Which means that the fabric is cut double, on one half of the chair. Using this method you can obtain an exact balance both with the pattern and with the lines of piping. Almost every type of furniture can be cut on the half. The exceptions are tub chairs, if they are very curved, and drop-end settees which are of course different on each arm. Any piece of furniture that is not identical each side, must be cut all over.

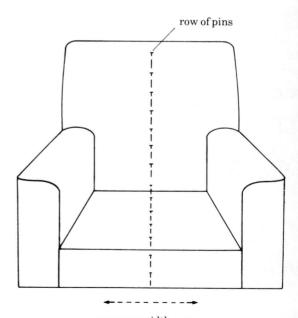

**265**

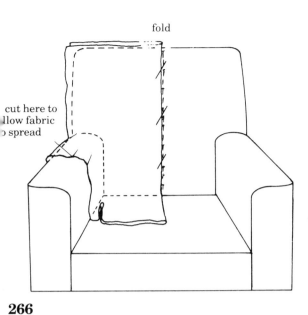

fold

cut here to
allow fabric
to spread

Using a tape measure mark with a straight line of pins, the exact halfway line, right down the middle of the chair. This must be accurate, as the chair cover will be too wide or narrow, depending on which side the cover has been cut. Check measurement both sides of the centre pin before proceeding **265.**

Starting with the fabric marked 'inside back'. Fold the fabric lengthways, exactly in half. Place on the chair, starting at the top of the back, and smoothing into position, pinning securely with the fold on the centre line of pins **266.**

**266**

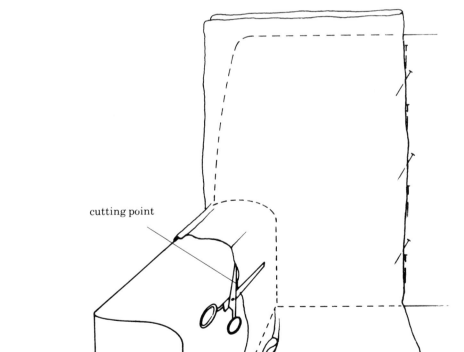

cutting point

**267** *Cut in an upward direction to allow fabric to spread round the top of the inside arm*

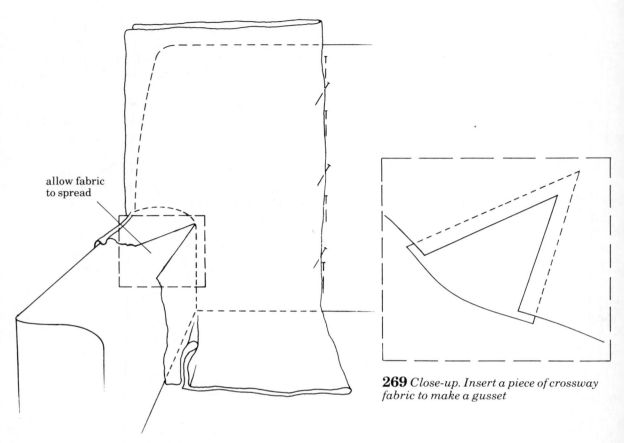

allow fabric
to spread

**269** *Close-up. Insert a piece of crossway fabric to make a gusset*

**268** *Fabric spread out into position ready to receive gusset*

Follow the instructions on the diagrams **267, 268, 269.** Then cut in an upward direction into the corner, where the inside back meets the top of the inside arm **270.**

Push fabric up and along top to form a dart at the top corner. Pin the dart from the outside edge. Trim surplus fabric to 1½ cm **271, 272.**

Place the seat fabric on the centre row of marking pins, in the same way as the inside back. Start at the front of the seat, leaving 1½ cm for turnings **273.**

Smooth the fabric towards the back of the chair, and pin the tuck-in section of inside back and seat together **274.**

Trim turnings to 1½ cm and notch along the edge (when machining the cover these notches match each other, and thus keep the cover in the correct position) **275.**

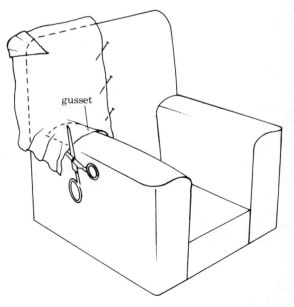

gusset

**270** *Make another cut into the corner, allowing fabric to spread round to meet the outside back*

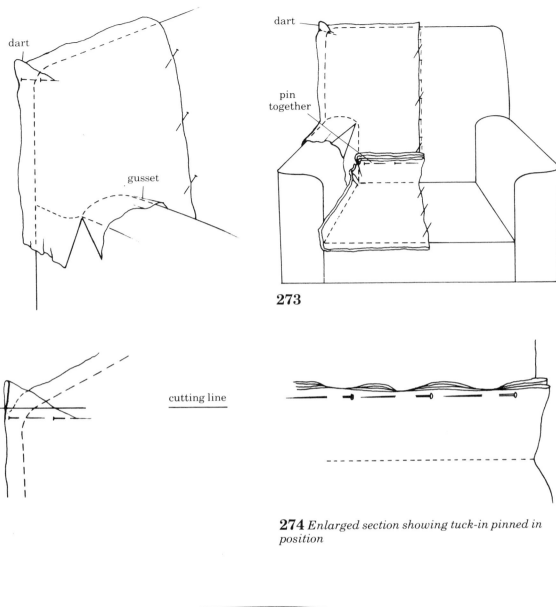

dart

gusset

**271**

**272**

cutting line

**273**

**274** *Enlarged section showing tuck-in pinned in position*

dart

pin together

**275** *Notches cut through four thicknesses of fabric*

With the wrong sides together, and making sure the patterns are upright, pin the inside arm in place. Leave at least 1½ cm turning at the front edge, and pin towards the back. Let the surplus fabric overlap the outside arm, this will be trimmed later when the outside arm is pinned in place **276**.

Smooth inside arm towards the back, and cut into the corners where it meets the inside back. This cut should match up to the corner cut already made in the inside back. Cut upwards so that enough fabric is left to spread round the corner, and give enough allowance for turnings **277, 278**.

Pin seat and inside arm tuck-in, together in the same manner as the seat and back. Pin tuck-in on the inside arms and inside back together pinning from the cut in the corner down to meet the seat section.

All three sections of the tuck-in should now be trimmed so that they meet. The surplus fabric in the corner of the seat where all sections meet, will tuck into the chair and spread out inside the chair, thus holding the cover in place **279**.

When the tuck-in has been trimmed and notched, push it into place down the inside of the chair **280**.

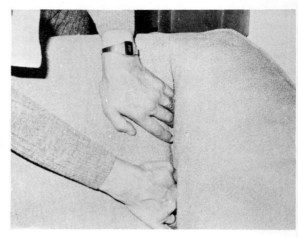

*Pushing the tuck-in into place*

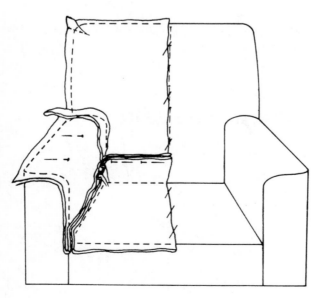

**276**

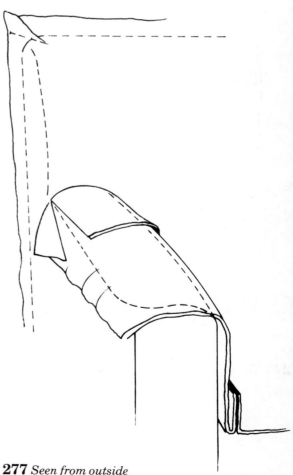

**277** *Seen from outside*

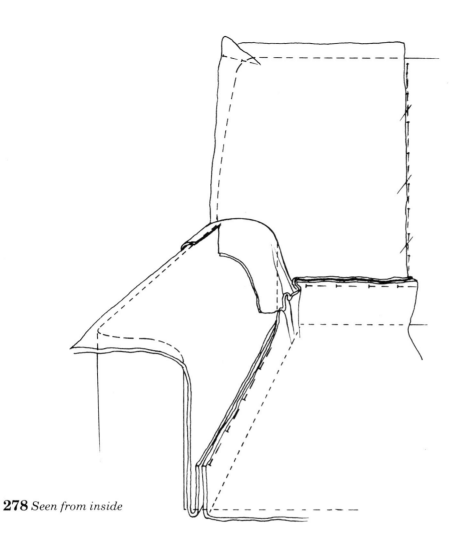

**278** *Seen from inside*

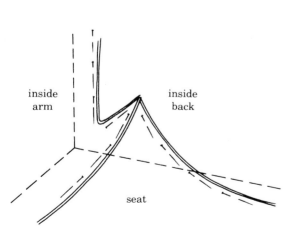

inside
arm

inside
back

seat

**279**

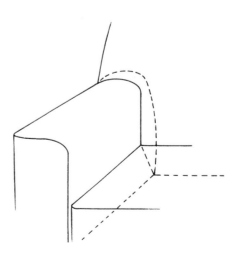

**280**

On some types of chair the base of the inside back and inside arms will not tuck in past the frame. If this occurs the fabric must be cut round the frame **281**.

When the tuck-in has been completed, the next stage is to pin the outside pieces in place. Leaving the $1\frac{1}{2}$ cm turning, fold the front border fabric lengthways and starting at the centre top follow the shape of the chair edge, snipping into the corner where the tuck-in turns into the seat. Mark with a cut where the tuck-in finishes. Trim and notch the turnings **282**.

Pin the outside arm starting at the front, and smoothing out towards the back. Keep the fabric straight along bottom edge, letting the surplus smooth towards the top edge.

Join the front border to the outside arm below the part where the tuck-in is marked. When the outside arm meets the inside arm, continue to pin along the line of the frame. Snip along the rounded edge to allow the fabric to spread **283, 284.**

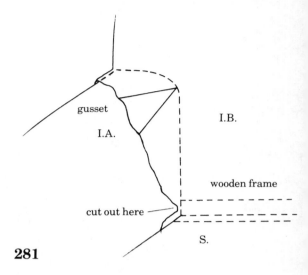

**281**

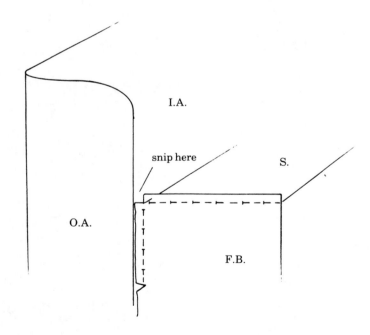

**282**

84

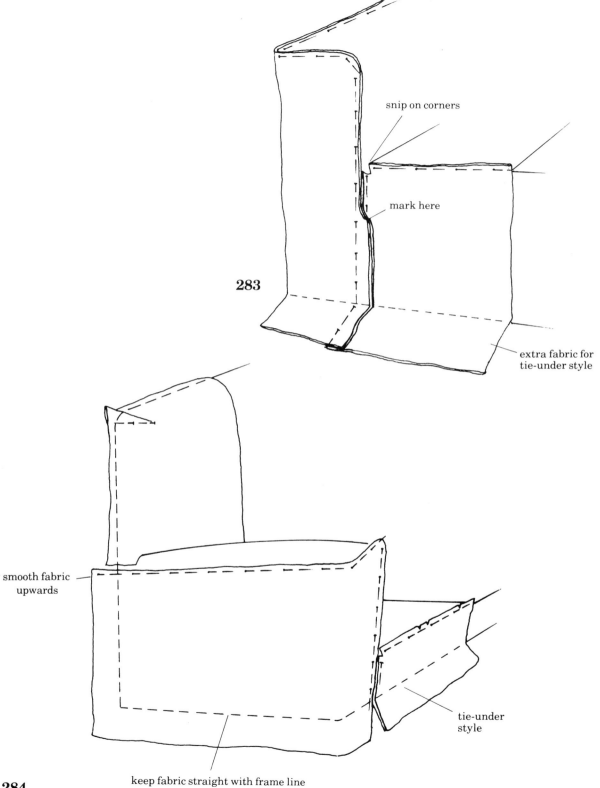

snip on corners

mark here

**283**

extra fabric for
tie-under style

smooth fabric
upwards

tie-under
style

**284**

keep fabric straight with frame line

Pin outside back to the inside back, starting at the top. Place the folded fabric along the centre line of pins, and fix into position. Keep the line of the fabric straight with the bottom edge of frame **285.**

Trim and notch the fabric, keeping to a $1\frac{1}{2}$ cm turning. To finish the chair cover in the tie-under style, turn the chair upside down and follow diagrams **286, 287, 288, 289.**

To finish the chair cover in a kick pleat style, or a box pleated style, measure from the floor up 15 cm and draw a line at this depth all round the base of the chair cover. Cut off $1\frac{1}{2}$ cm below this line, to allow for turning. Cut lengths required for pleating (see *base finishes* page 78).

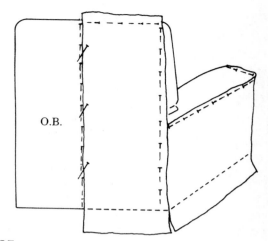

O.B.

**285**

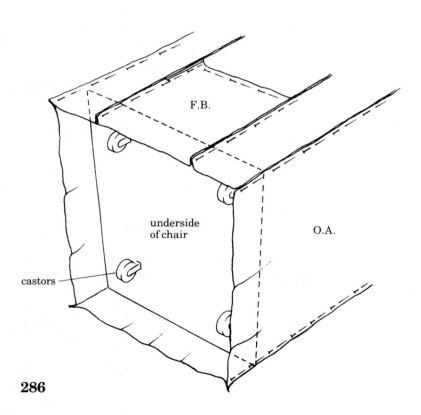

F.B.

underside of chair

castors

O.A.

**286**

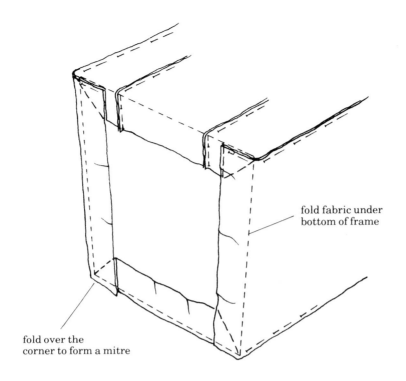

fold fabric under
bottom of frame

fold over the
corner to form a mitre

**287**

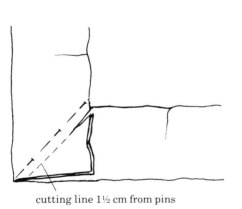

cutting line 1½ cm from pins

**288**

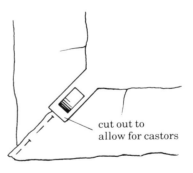

cut out to
allow for castors

**289**

# 14: Assembling a loose cover

Having cut out all the pieces for your loose cover you may feel as if you have an impossible jig-saw puzzle to solve, but it is not difficult when you know how. There are also instructions for finishing the base of your cover in different ways.

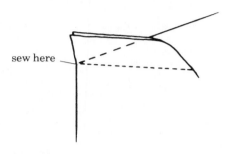

**290** *Sewing the dart*

Having cut the loose cover, cut and prepare enough piping to pipe all the outside edges on the cover (see *Cutting and making piping* Chapter 11).

Unpin all the outside pieces, and lay them to one side. Now unpin the tuck-in section. This consists of the inside back, seat and inside arms. With a chair that has a gusset and darts, sew these first, making sure the ends of the darts finish smoothly **290, 291.**

Press the darts out at this stage, as they are very much easier to press while flat. Place the seat section right side up and put the inside back face down on to it so that the notches match. Machine along this line and then neaten the edge, by oversewing or double stitching **292.**

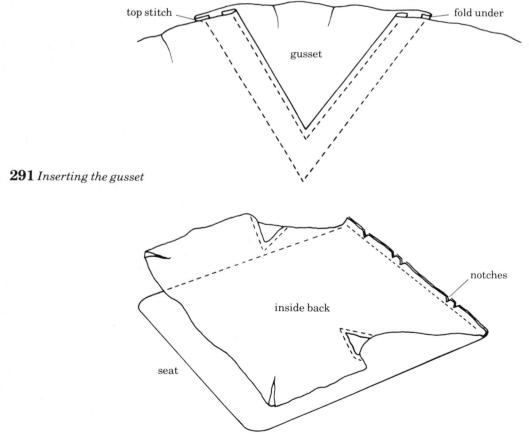

**291** *Inserting the gusset*

**292** *Attaching inside back to seat*

Next pin the inside arms in place, matching
the notches. Start machining at the front of
the seat. Match the seam. Now join the inside
back and arm, starting from the top of the
arm **293**.

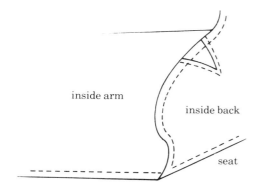

**293**

When the tuck-in has been assembled, leave
it to one side and start to pipe the outside
pieces. Before piping think where the lines
are going to be on the chair. A continuous
line looks much better than a broken one
**294, 295**.

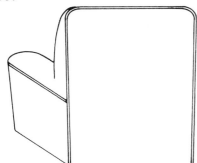

**294** *Line unbroken (right)*

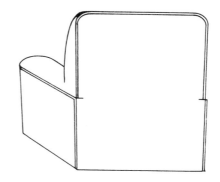

**295** *Line broken (wrong)*

The chair in the drawing is piped as follows:
front border, outside arms, outside back
(with the one-sided zip foot or a grooved
piping foot) **296, 297, 298**.

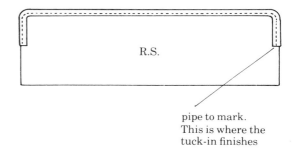

**296** *Front border*

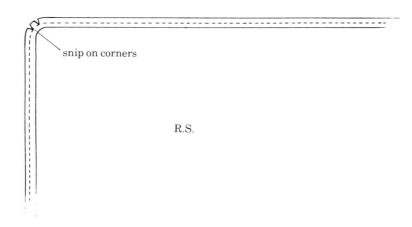

**297** *Outside arms*

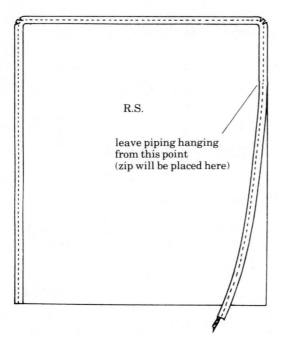

R.S.

leave piping hanging
from this point
(zip will be placed here)

**298** *Outside back*

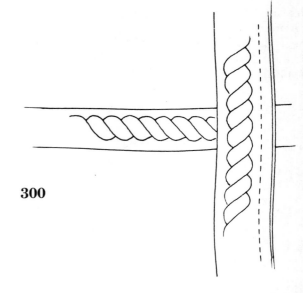

**300**

When pieces have been piped, join each
piece to the tuck-in, starting with the front
border. Place the right sides together, and
keep as close to the cord as possible, so that
none of the previous stitching can be seen
from the right side **299**.

Where two lengths of piping overlap, cut the
cord in the underneath length back to where
the stitching line crosses it so that the top
piping will lie flat **300**.

Once the cover has been assembled, the zip
must be sewn into the opening left between
the outside back and inside back and outside
arm. The piece of piping that was left hanging
is now sewn onto the inside back and outside
arm section **301**, **302**.

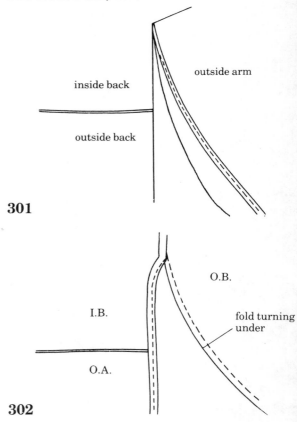

inside back

outside arm

outside back

**301**

I.B.

O.B.

O.A.

fold turning
under

**302**

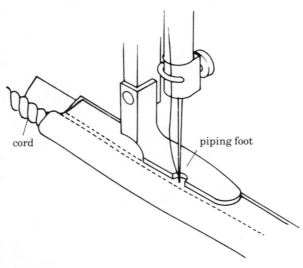

cord

piping foot

**299** *Stitch detail*

The closed zip, is now placed under this opening, with the zip end at the base of the cover. Fold the turning on the outside back under and pin the zip in place **303.**

Machine the zip in place. Hide the stitching line in the piping on the piped side. Make a neat straight line of stitching on the plain side. When closed the piping should cover the zip, making it invisible **304.**

**To finish the tie-under style cover** Tape back all the cut-out sections, where the castors will be protruding.

Use 1½ cm straight tape (or crossway strips of the same fabric as the cover may be used) **305, 306.**

At the corners mitre the tape so that it lies flat **307.**

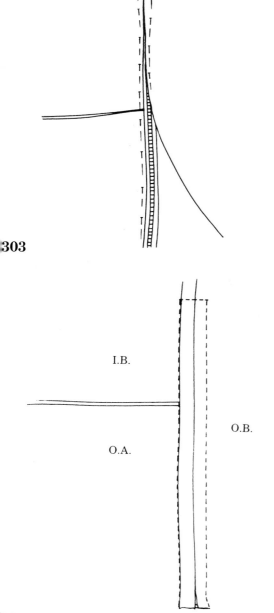

**303**

**304** *Stitching the zip in place*

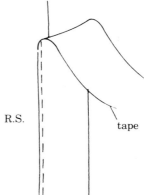

**305** *Taping back, step one*

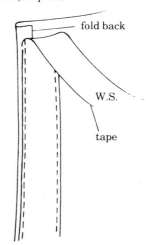

**306** *Taping back, step two*

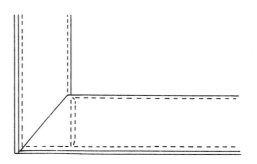

**307** *Taping back, mitring the corners*

After taping all the cut-outs, turn the bottom edge of the cover up to form a hem. This hem needs to be approximately 3 cm deep to allow a tape to be threaded through **308**.

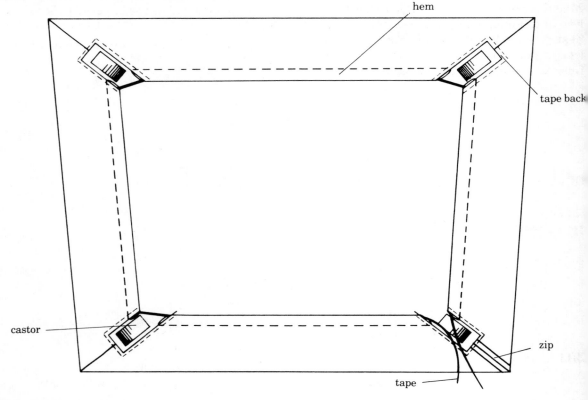

**308** *Threading the tape through the chair hem*

**To finish the chair in a kick pleat style or box pleated style** Measure from the floor up 15 cm and draw a line at this depth all round the base of the chair cover. Cut off 1½ cm below this line to allow for turnings **309**

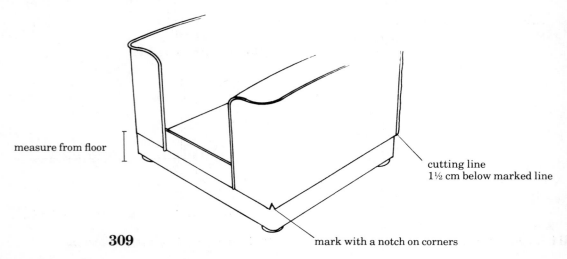

**309**

Stitch the strips of fabric together. For the kick pleat style seam at each corner, allowing enough fabric to pleat underneath (approximately 10 cm). Line the front section up with the front border if using patterned fabric.

The kick pleat will lie much better if it is lined. The lining is stitched together in strips in the same way as the fabric, and then stitched to the fabric at the base, right sides together **310, 311, 312, 313.**

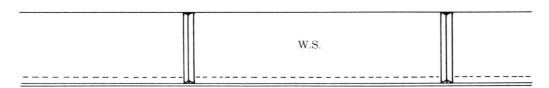

**310** *Joining pleat to lining at the bottom edge*

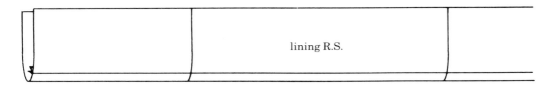

**311** *Seam folded up so that 2 cm of fabric shows on the lining side*

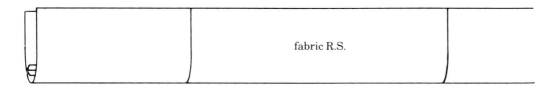

**312** *Pleat from the right side*

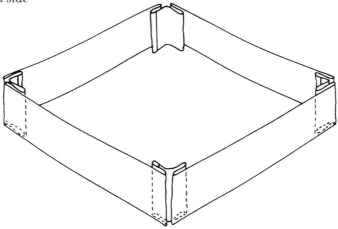

**313** *Kick pleating assembled before attaching to loose cover*

**Box pleat style**   The box pleats may be unlined, so, after joining the pieces to form one long strip, hem the bottom edge. A hem of $2\frac{1}{2}$ cm is sufficient. Machine the hem, and then proceed to fold the pleats. Fold at a distance of 5 cm intervals (that is 5 cm pleat, 5 cm space). Machine the pleats in place along the top edge **314.**

**To finish either style**   Having prepared the pleats or kick pleat, the next step is to pipe all round the base of the cover. Start and finish at the back opening. Fold the ends of the piping in to make a neat finish on the ends **315.**

Pin the pleats onto the piped base, lining up the kick pleats with the corner notches. The box pleats must start with a pleat and end with a space, so that they continue in sequence when the cover is on. For either style, fold the pleat round at the beginning and end so that the end of the base seam is covered. Machine in place and neaten the raw edges **316.**

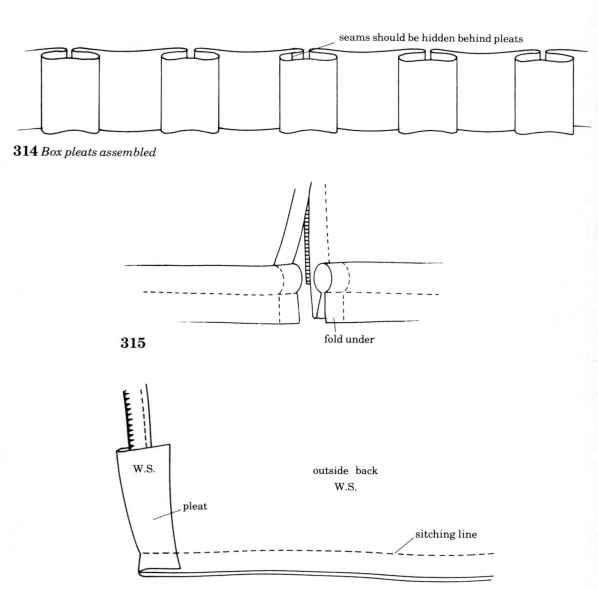

seams should be hidden behind pleats

**314** *Box pleats assembled*

**315**

fold under

W.S.

outside  back
W.S.

pleat

sitching line

**316**

The cover is now ready to press and fit onto the chair. Always fit the back of the cover first, then pull the arms over the front of the chair.

Push the tuck-in away down the sides and back until all of the cover is lying smoothly. Turn the piping so that all the seams are lying flat, and zip up the cover. If it is a tie-under style, pull the tape as tightly as possible and tie in a double bow. Do not cut any excess tape away, but tuck it under the cover.

When re-fitting loose covers after washing, fit onto the chair while slightly damp. This will help the cover to dry into shape **317.**

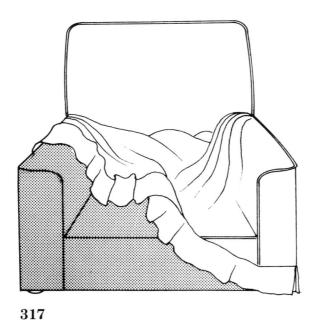

**317**

# 15: Loose covers for fireside chairs

The main difference between a fireside chair and an easy chair is that usually there is no tuck-in on a fireside chair.

To begin the cutting, the chair must be halved, as shown in Chapter 13 for the easy chair 318.

Measure and cut off the length required in exactly the same manner as for the easy chair. After cutting the lengths, proceed to pin the inside back in position on the halfway mark (folded lengthwise as for the easy chair). Next place the seat in position and fix it with a few pins. Join the two pieces where they meet at the back of the seat, trim to $1\frac{1}{2}$ cm 319.

Pin the back border in place, and proceed to pin along the shape of the frame line. The two back borders must be paired so that when they are opened out they are a right and a left side 320.

To cut round the wooden arm, requires great care, as it must be exactly right. Where the wooden arm is joined to the chair back the fabric must be cut to fit round it. Cut at an angle as shown in diagram. Tape back cut edges to neaten (for taping back see page 91) 321, 322.

Continue to pin the back and back border until they meet the seat. Trim and notch the seam. Pin the front border and the side border in place. (The side border will have to be cut round the wooden leg in the same manner as the arm). Pin on the outside back. Trim all seams and notch 323.

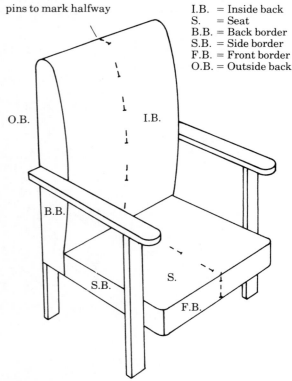

pins to mark halfway

I.B. = Inside back
S. = Seat
B.B. = Back border
S.B. = Side border
F.B. = Front border
O.B. = Outside back

O.B.     I.B.

B.B.

S.B.     S.

F.B.

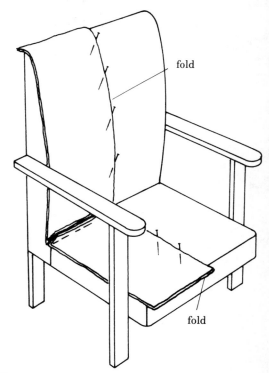

fold

fold

**318** *Parts of a fireside chair*     **319**

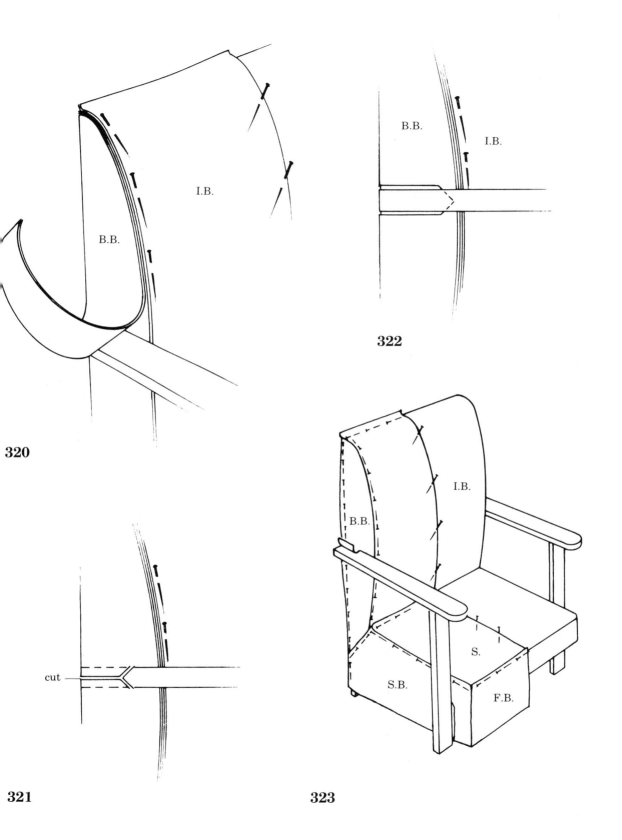

**320**

**322**

**321**

**323**

Turn chair upside down, and cut fabric round the legs **324.**

To assemble the loose cover for the fireside chair, proceed in exactly the same manner as for the easy chair (see Chapter 14), starting with the inside section. To allow for the protruding wooden arms the outside back must be opened both sides. Velcro is usually the best type of opening to use on a fireside chair, but an open ended zip could be used **325.**

The underneath is taped back and hemmed in the same manner as the tie-under easy chair (see Chapter 14). There are many types of fireside chair; the following diagram shows the method of cutting on one of the most common types, one with a covered back and sides and a separate cushion **326.**

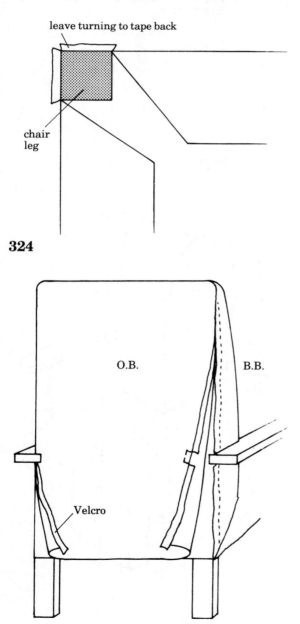

**324**

**325**

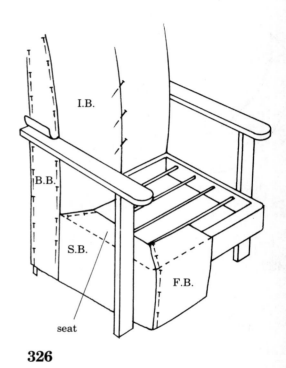

**326**

# Types of opening

So far in this book we have concentrated mostly on using zips for opening and closing seams, however, here are some alternatives to use when a different treatment is called for.

**Velcro** is very useful on fireside chairs as it enables the seam to open at both ends **327, 328, 329, 330.**

Make sure that the Velcro is paired (one side is rough and one side is fluffy), otherwise it will not adhere.

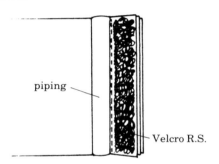

**327** *Fluffy side of Velcro attached to seam allowance*

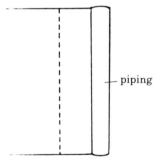

**328** *Fluffy side of Velcro turned to inside and stitched in place*

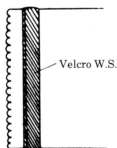

**329** *Hooked (or rough) side of Velcro stitched to cover, right sides facing*

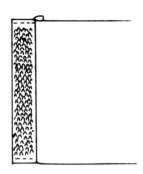

**330** *Seam allowance turned to inside so that Velcro extends beyond edge of cover. Top stitch in place*

## Placket

A placket opening is made using the same fabric, as that used for the cover. To fasten it hooks and eyes or press studs may be used **331, 332, 333, 334.**

This type of opening can be used either with both ends open or one end closed, or with both ends closed (e.g. cushion closure).

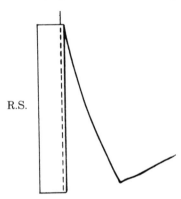

**331** *Attach strip of fabric to one side of opening, right sides facing*

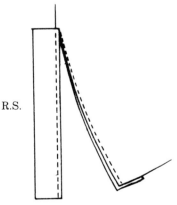

**332** *Attach second strip of fabric to other side of opening, right side of strip to wrong side of fabric*

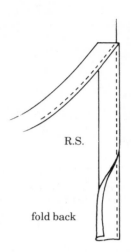

**333** *Turn second strip to right side, turn in raw edge and stitch in place*

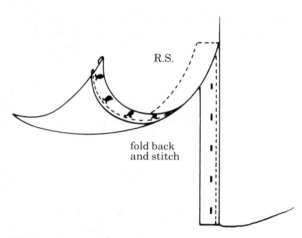

**334** *Turn first strip to wrong side, turn in raw edge and stitch in place. Sew on hooks and eyes by hand*

## Pillow type

Sometimes known as *housewife style*, this type of opening is used on cushions, pillow slips and occasionally on duvets. Allow an extra 4 cm on side one, and an extra 18 cm on side two to fold back. The pillow is inserted into the case, and tucked under the flap, usually this opening would be used without hooks or fasteners **335, 336, 337.**

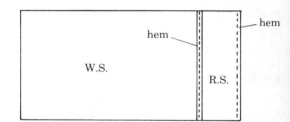

**335** *Turn under 2 cm and then 2 cm again to make hems on both long and short sides*

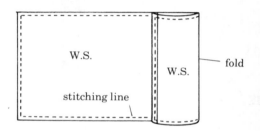

**336** *Fold back longer side over short side and machine round all three edges*

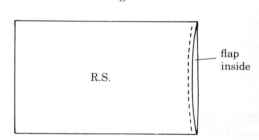

**337** *Turn right side out*

# 16: Duvets and bed bases

## Cutting and making a duvet

Duvets (or continental quilts) have been used on the continent for many years. Now they are becoming increasingly popular here. They are very light and warm, especially if the filling is goose or eider down. Modern man-made fillings have their advantages, as they are washable as well as lightweight and they are, of course, cheaper than down-filled duvets. The duvet has a channelled construction, which gives good insulation and this is achieved by inserting gussets down the whole length of the quilt **338**.

When calculating the amount of fabric required, a good guide is to add an extra 45 cm *each* side to the measurement of the bed width. The minimum would be 30 cm *each* side. The length of a duvet for the average size bed should be 2 metres. If the bed is extra long, add extra length accordingly. The best fabric to use for a duvet is downproof cambric, usually off white, although it can be obtained in other colours **339.**

Mark up the fabric for the gussets, divide the duvet across the width into equal sections, each section being not more than 40 cm wide. (Add extra gussets rather than make the sections too large). Mark the sections at either end on the wrong side of the fabric, then join up the markings by drawing lines the whole length of the duvet. Mark the two layers of the duvet on the wrong side of the fabric. After marking, crease each line along its entire length.

**338** *Cross section of a duvet*

**339** *Cutting plan for a single size duvet*

Place the two layers of the duvet together, right sides facing, then stitch the two long edges together. With the wrong sides out, attach the gusset to either side of the duvet, shape the gussets to a point at either end (shown in diagram). This is to eliminate bulk at the top and bottom of the quilt **340**.

Continue stitching gussets, until they are all in place. Turn the duvet right side out. Fold in the bottom edge, and seam together with two rows of stitching **341**.

Fill the case with down (or your chosen filling), making sure that each channel has the same quantity of filling. When filled, turn in the top edge, and seam together with two rows of stitching. Cut a length of tape approximately 10 cm long. Fold this in half and stitch a length to each corner to form a loop. This is to hold the duvet in place inside the cover **342**.

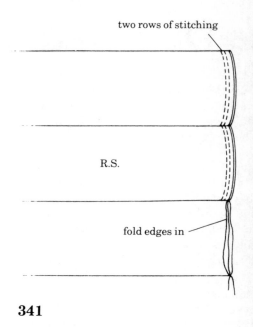

two rows of stitching

R.S.

fold edges in

**341**

**342**

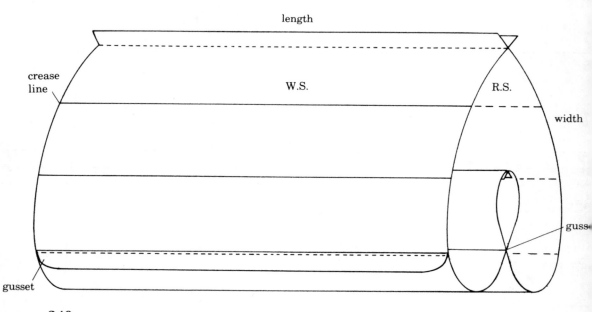

length

crease line

W.S.

R.S.

width

gusset

gusset

**340**

102

## Duvet outer cover

Using the same cutting plan as for the actual duvet, cut a top and underside. If piping is to be used on the edges cut this now. With a patterned fabric, the design must be centralised. If the fabric is not wide enough, a seam must be made either side of the central width, *never* down the middle. After cutting the main sections, seam these together down one side, leaving a gap in the middle to insert the zip. If the duvet cover is to be piped, pipe the top layer (see Chapter 11) before joining the side seam **343**.

Press the seam open and place the zip in position. Sew one side of the zip in place from the wrong side of the fabric, stitching through the seam allowance only and keeping the other layers of fabric free **344**. Stitch the other side of the zip in exactly the same way, keeping the fabric clear of the seam. Over-sew by hand at the ends of the zip to make it secure. The zip will now be invisible from the right side **345**.

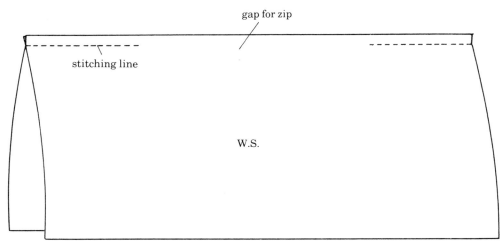

**343**

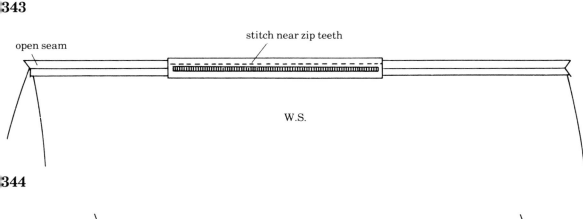

**344**

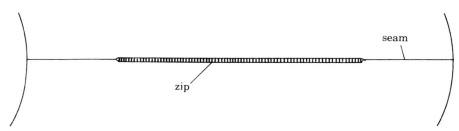

**345**

After inserting the zip, continue seaming the sides top and bottom. On each corner sew in a double tape approximately 18 cm long. These tapes can then be tied through the loops at the corners of the duvet so that it will keep the duvet in the corners and prevent it from riding inside the cover **346.**

After completing the seams, neaten all the raw edges and press. Attach the duvet to the cover with the ties, turn the complete duvet and cover right side out and zip up the side **347.**

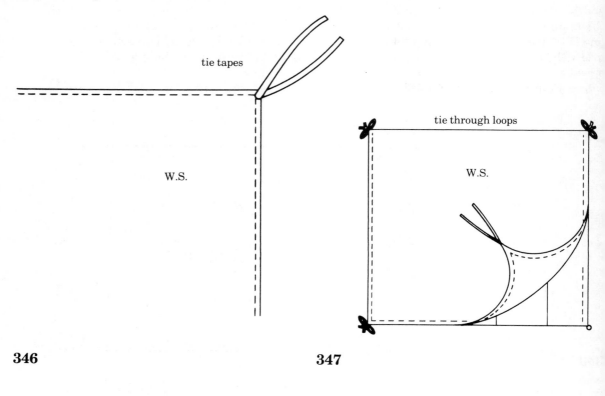

**346**

**347**

# Bed bases

The cover on a bed base does not get as much handling as a bedcover or duvet as it stays in place until it is washed or dry cleaned. The mattress holds the cover in place, but it can also be tied at each corner to keep it from slipping about. These bases have become very popular when used with a duvet in either matching or contrasting fabric. They can be made in several different styles: the two following are the most popular. In both cases lining is used to cover the whole bed base and the main fabric is attached to the lining round the edges to form a border. The frill or kick pleat is attached to both layers **348, 349.**

The frill usually goes round three sides only, as the top end is usually against a wall or a headboard. If, however, the bed is in the middle of the room, allow extra fabric to make the frill all round. An average amount of fabric widths for a single bed would be seven of 122 cm width fabric. A double bed would take nine widths of 122 cm width fabric. This allows double fullness for a gathered frill. The kick pleat style would take four widths for a single bed (and six for a double bed) of 122 cm width fabric. For this width fabric you will need to make a seam in each side section.

The gathered frill may be unlined if the fabric is fairly heavy, otherwise it will hang better if it is lined. The kick pleat is generally lined, unless the fabric is exceptionally heavy, in which case it would be hemmed by hand.

**Assembling the base**  Seam up the side strips and cut to size. Place on the lining, with the wrong side of the fabric to the right side of the lining. Place the end strips in the same manner and allow them to overlap the side strips. Cut these off level with the outer edge of the lining **350.**

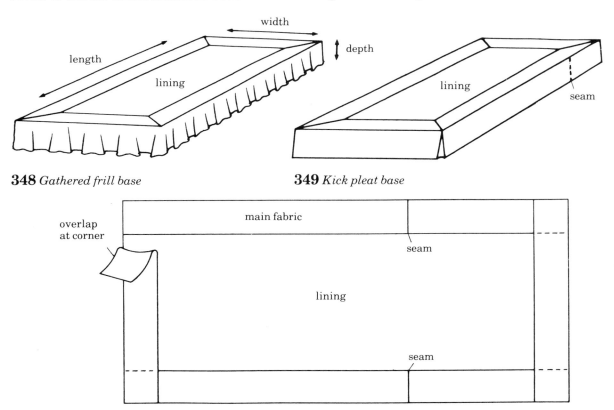

**348** *Gathered frill base*

**349** *Kick pleat base*

**350** *Assembling the base*

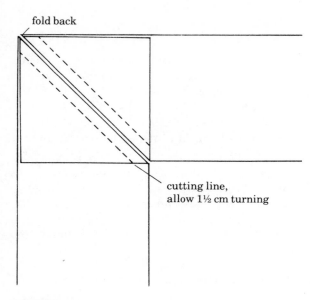

fold back

cutting line,
allow 1½ cm turning

Pin the strips to outer edge of the lining. Mitre the corners **351**.

Turn in the inner edge of the main fabric and top stitch to the lining all round. Top stitch the outer edges (which are raw) with a long zigzag stitch. This is just to hold the two layers together in preparation for applying the frill or kick pleat.

Join the frill sections in one length, if the frill is unlined, turn in the side edges and hem, then turn up the bottom hem 1 cm, then 4 cm and stitch in place by hand **352**.

**Lined frill**   After joining the sections of fabric in one length, seam the lining in the same manner. With right sides facing, machine along the lower edge taking $1\frac{1}{2}$ cm turning **353**.

**351** *Mitring the corners. Open out one seam allowance and top stitch the other edge in place over it*

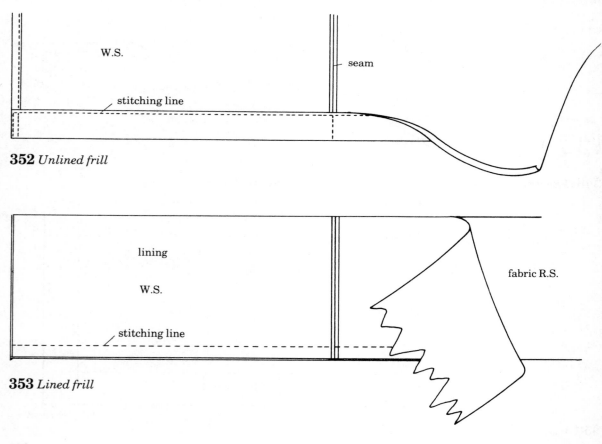

W.S.

seam

stitching line

**352** *Unlined frill*

lining

W.S.

fabric R.S.

stitching line

**353** *Lined frill*

Turn right side out and fold back the lining until 3 cm of main fabric is showing. Press the edge and turn in the two ends, slipstitch in place **354.**

Measure to the depth required, adding the 1½ cm turning. Trim to size, and tack along the top edge to prevent the two edges from moving. If this process is not done the lining moves along, and a twist develops, making the frill hang badly **355.**

If the frill is to be gathered, measure halfway along the top and put in a notch, then a quarter along and mark with another notch, until there are four even sections along the top. Gather each section between the notches either by hand or machine **356.**

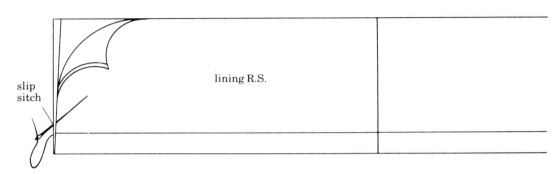

**354** *Lined frill*

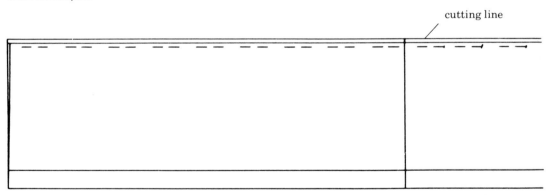

**355** *Lined frill*

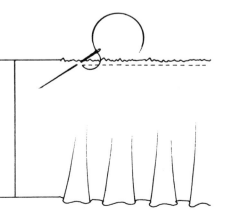

**356**

Halve and quarter the bedcover, on the three sides to which the frill will be attached. Notch in the same manner.

If the bed base has a kick pleat style, halve the frill section and notch the centre. Then halve the bottom edge of the base and notch this in the centre. Pin into position starting at the top edge. Where the pleat meets on the corner, fold under, thus concealing the seams **357.**

If the frill is gathered, space these out evenly, between the notches and attach to the top of the bed base on three sides **358.**

Stitch all round, trim and neaten the raw edges. Tape back the top edge of the base cover. Press all over and place on the bed base. Place the mattress over the bed base cover.

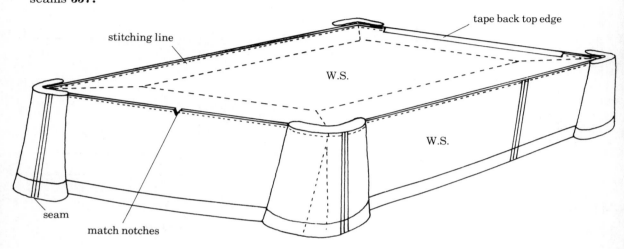

**357** *Kick pleat style*

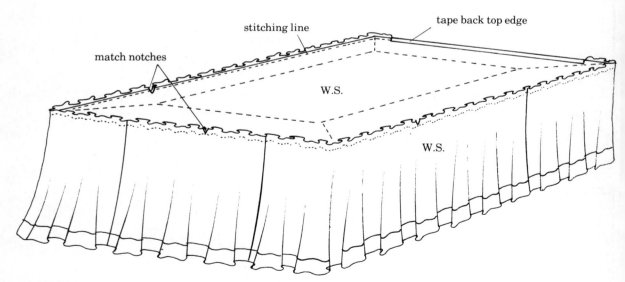

**358** *Gathered frill style*

# 17: **Bedcovers**

Bedcovers made with a gusset or flap to allow for pillows have a professional look.

## Bedcover with a gusset

The gusset is used on the bedcover to take up the extra height created by the pillows. The length of the gusset is on average 40 cm. The depth depends on how many pillows are used **359**.

When cutting out, the extra length must be added to the measurement of the bed top to allow for the insertion of the gusset and an extra 15 cm to tuck under the pillow. Make sure to cut a *pair* of gussets, one for each side. Make an allowance of 6 cm for hems on each frill section, and $1\frac{1}{2}$ cm turning on all the seams. When making a double size bedcover, the fabric must be joined along the selvedge edge on either side of the main section, to make up the full width of the bed **360**.

Cut and join the piping. Pipe the base of each gusset. Pipe the bedcover top, starting at the top right hand side, and finishing at the top left hand side **361, 362.**

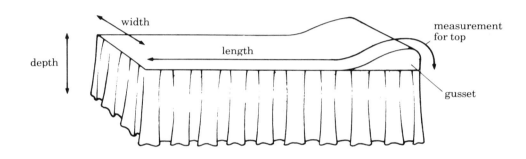

**359**

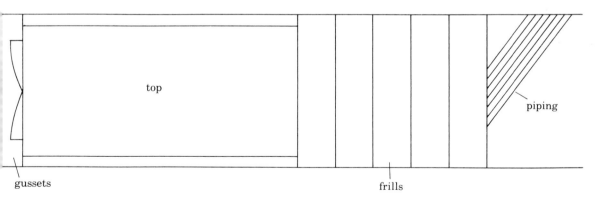

**360** *Cutting plan for bedcover with gussets*

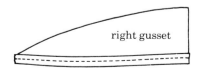

**361** *Piping the gussets*

109

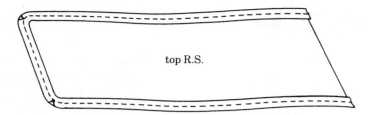

**362** *Piping the bedcover*

Pin the gussets in position, and stitch to the piped edge of the bedcover **363.**

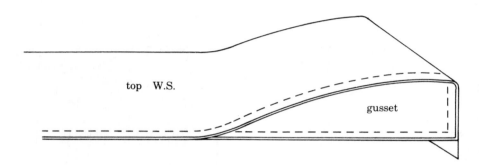

**363**

Make up the frill or kick pleat in the same manner as for the bed bases (page 106). Stitch the frill to the top of the bedcover and the lower edge of the gusset **364.**

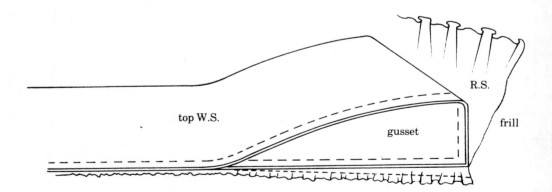

**364**

To line the bedcover top, place the bedcover
wrong side down on the table, with the frill
lying towards the centre **365.**

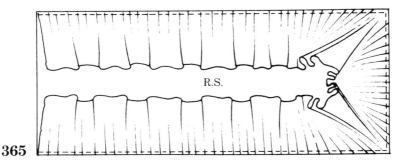

365

Cut the lining to the same size as the main
top fabric, and place it right side down onto
the bedcover. Pin into position and machine
all round, leaving a gap on the bottom edge
to enable the cover to be turned right side out.
Turn the cover right side out, slipstitch the
opening **366.**

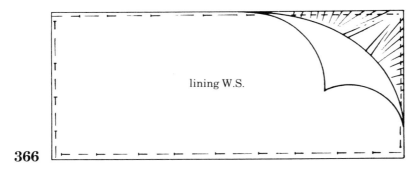

366

To line the gusset, pin the lining in position,
turning under the edges as you pin. Slipstitch
into place using slipping thread. Keep the
stitches small and even as this area of the
bedcover has a lot of handling when it is
removed or folded back **367.**

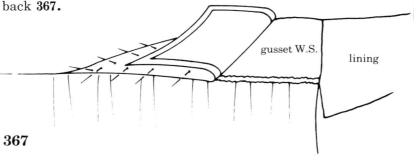

367

# Bedcover with top flap

This type of bedcover is made in exactly the
same manner as the previous bedcover with
the omission of the gusset. Make the
bedcover and line it, but this time the lining
should be sewn only down the two sides and
bottom, leaving the whole top edge open 368.

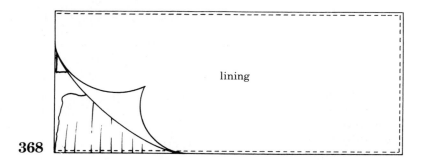

To make the flap, cut a length of fabric,
approximately 90 cm long. The width should
be approximately 30 cm wider than the bed
width *each* side. Cut the lining exactly the
same size, and place the two pieces together,
right sides facing. Use notches to mark the
width of the bedcover top in the centre of the
flap 369.

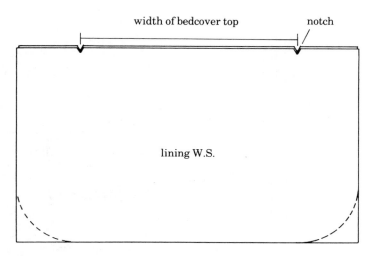

**369** *Bedcover flap. Round off corners before stitching, if required*

Stitch all round the area between the notches. Turn right side out and press. Place the flap on top of the bedcover, so that the right sides of both are facing up. Stitch the flap to the main part of the lined bedcover leaving the flap lining free and finishing the seam at the frilled edges **370.**

Open out and place the bedcover with the right side up on the table. Fold the lining on the flap under and slipstitch in place, along the stitch line of the flap seam **371.**

Press bedcover all over and place on the bed. Place the pillows directly onto the cover, and fold the flap back to cover them. The flap can either be tucked right under pillows to look like a bolster or can be left flat.

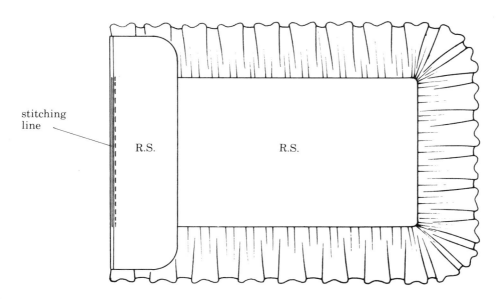

stitching
line

R.S.

R.S.

**370**

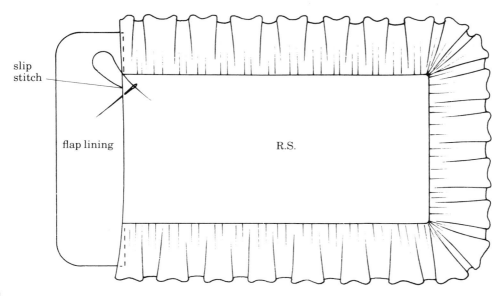

slip
stitch

flap lining

R.S.

**371**

# 18: Quilting

Quilting can be used purely as decoration, or for decoration and warmth. A light thin fabric may be thickly padded making a warm but elegant covering fabric. There are several types of quilting, here we show how to do some of them.

## English quilting
Used mainly for bed coverings and stools, this type is padded throughout with wadding. The stitching passes right through the layers of fabric and padding.

To begin quilting, lay the muslin flat, place the wadding on top, then lay the fabric on top of the wadding. An allowance of at least $2\frac{1}{2}$ cm to every 30 cm should be made, when cutting the fabric, as the stitching takes up this amount. Always cut the finished measurement after the quilting has been completed. To quilt with a straight machine stitch the three layers must be tacked together to keep them from moving under the machine foot **372**.

After completing the tacking, measure up 15 cm from the bottom corner and make a mark with tailor's chalk. Measure in the same manner along the bottom edge and mark. With a straight rule draw a line across to give a 45° angle. Tack along this line **373**.

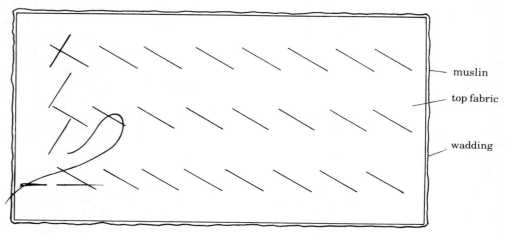

muslin

top fabric

wadding

**372** *Tack across and down at 15 cm intervals*

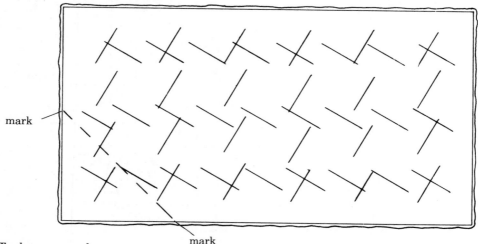

mark

mark

**373** *Tack across angle*

114

To quilt in a diamond pattern, machine along the tacking line. Starting at the same edge again, measure 8 cm from the machine line and using a quilting gauge keep the stitching exactly 8 cm from the first line. Continue until all the lines are stitched across. A piece of card cut to size can be used as a gauge **374.**

After completing all the lines one way, mark the opposite corner at the 45° angle and quilt as before, crossing the first row of lines to form diamonds **375.**

When all the diamonds have been formed, remove all the tacking threads, and cut the quilting to the size required. The underside of the quilting should be lined on the finished article.

Different designs may be drawn onto the muslin underneath and tacked through to the top side instead of diamonds. It is sometimes necessary to use tissue paper to protect both the top fabric and the muslin when stitching.

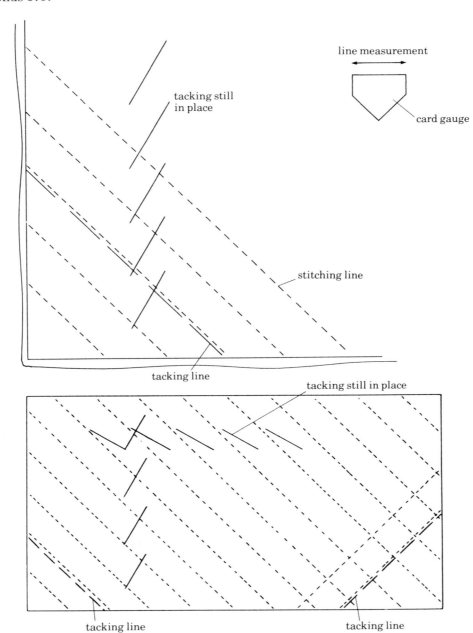

line measurement

tacking still in place

card gauge

stitching line

tacking line

**374**

tacking still in place

tacking line

tacking line

**375**

115

## Italian quilting

This type of quilting has no wadding at the back and the stitching is usually done by hand. A transfer of the design is applied to the muslin backing. This is then tacked on to the underside of the fabric. Tack in the same manner as for English quilting.

The designs in Italian quilting run in double lines, the channel in the centre is raised by threading a neutral coloured tapestry thread, between the muslin and top fabric 376.

Stitch through the muslin and top fabric with a small running stitch, keeping the stitches in line. Sew along the parallel lines, leaving a centre channel 377.

After completing the design, thread a bodkin with tapestry wool. This wool should then be threaded through the channel, leaving a loop of wool on the wrong side every 8 cm. This will allow the quilting to lie flat when pressed, if the wool is pulled tight the quilting will pucker 378.

When completed, press carefully, easing all the puckers out. The quilting is then ready to be cut to size.

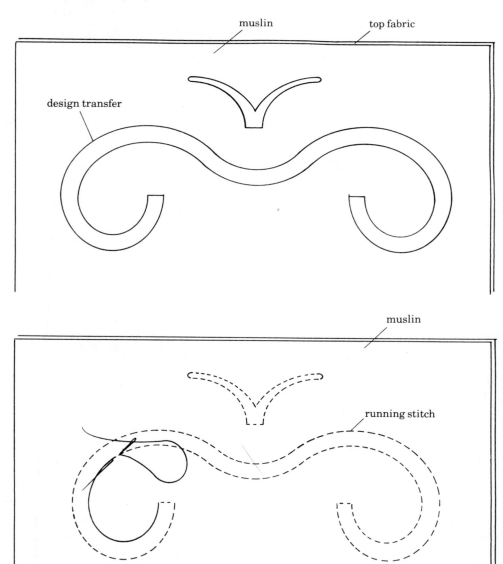

muslin

top fabric

design transfer

376

muslin

running stitch

377

116

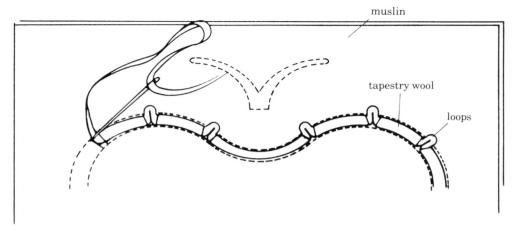

muslin

tapestry wool

loops

**378**

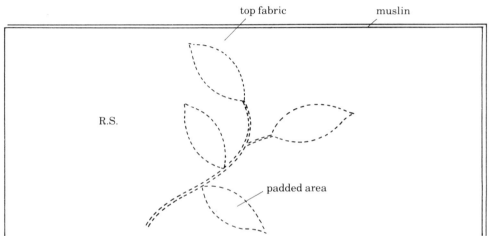

top fabric

muslin

R.S.

padded area

**379** *Trapunto quilting, right side*

## Trapunto quilting

This type of quilting is not padded all over, certain areas are outlined with a running stitch and padded from the underside. To quilt in this manner, the fabric must be backed with muslin and this must be tacked so that the two materials are held firmly together. The design can be drawn on the underside of the muslin, or on to the top fabric. The areas to be padded are outlined with a running stitch or if stitched from the topside a chain stitch may be used. This type of quilting is used with embroidery and is purely decorative **379**.

The muslin on the back of the padded area is now slit open and the padding inserted. The muslin is then stitched back together **380**.

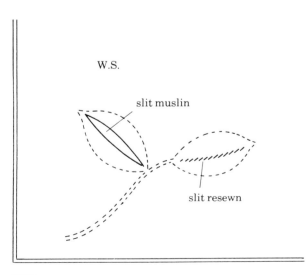

W.S.

slit muslin

slit resewn

**380** *Trapunto quilting, wrong side*

117

# Recovering an eiderdown

Recovering an eiderdown is not an economical proposition unless it has a very good filling and a sound inner cover. However, if you are convinced that it has both of these then you can make it look as good as new. First of all it is best to have the eiderdown dry cleaned. Then strip off all the old cover, which has probably started to shred. Cut close to the stitching lines and the fabric will pull away. Do not undo the machine stitching, as this design can be restitched on the new fabric. Most eiderdowns have a central section and an outer border **381**.

Having stripped off all the outer covering, decide at this stage whether to copy the original design or draw a new one (if you decide on a *new* design, the stitching of the centre section must be carefully removed). If the original design is being used, place a sheet of tissue paper over the central section and pin in place, making sure the eiderdown is pulled out as flat as possible. This is to ensure that the end result is the same size as the original.

The reason for using tissue paper instead of drawing direct to the fabric is that pencil or chalk marks are not easily removed from fine

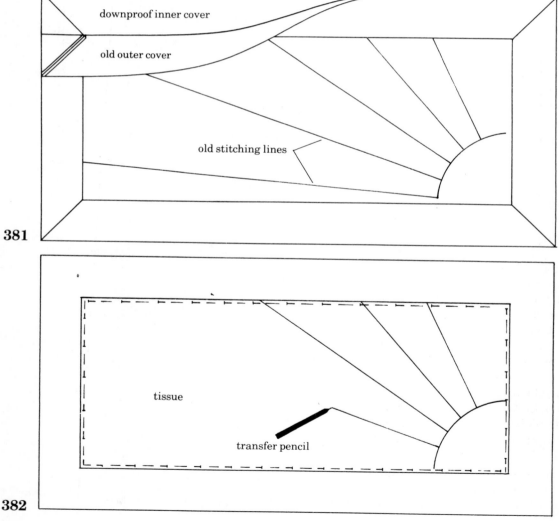

downproof inner cover

old outer cover

old stitching lines

**381**

tissue

transfer pencil

**382**

fabrics and may not be concealed by the final stitching. With practice and a simple design, it is possible to 'feel' the design through the top fabric and thus pin in place. However, this is not recommended for a beginner. Once the tissue paper has been pinned in place, mark the design carefully with a transfer pencil, or chalk. After drawing the design, remove the tissue and keep it to one side until needed **382**.

The next stage is to measure and cut the cover. First measure the centre section on the top side of the eiderdown, both across and along the length, add turnings of $1\frac{1}{2}$ cm all round.

Next, measure the side, top and bottom borders, both in length and width, and add $1\frac{1}{2}$ cm turnings. The underside is not usually mitred on the corners, as it is a non-slip backing of downproof sateen in a toning colour. The downproof is not always made as wide as the top fabric, if it has to be joined to make up the width, the seam must go on either side of the main width.

A patterned fabric must be centralised, and if an eiderdown is to be reversible the underside is cut and assembled in the same manner as the top side. Join the side sections to the centre back section, with selvedge edges together. Press the seams open flat. The back is now ready to use, once the top section has been completed.

Lay the side and end sections of the eiderdown top, right side down, on the table in their correct positions.

Fold back the corners, at right angles, and tack across from inside to outside corners. Machine across, and trim the seam to $1\frac{1}{2}$ cm **383, 384**.

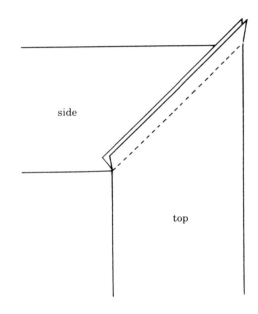

**384** *Detail of mitred corner*

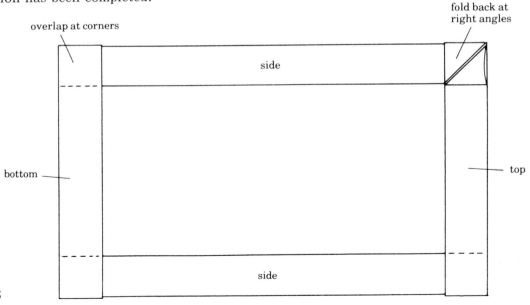

After completing all the corners. Lay the centre section in place, right side down and pin into position **385.**

Machine stitch all round and press all the seams open. Pipe (or ruche) all round the outer edge of the top side of the eiderdown, starting and ending halfway along the side (see Chapter 11). Place the piped top side on to the underside, right sides facing. Stitch together round the outside leaving an opening of approximately 60 cm halfway along the side section **386.**

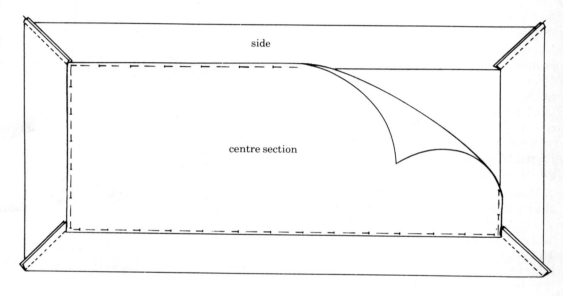

**385**

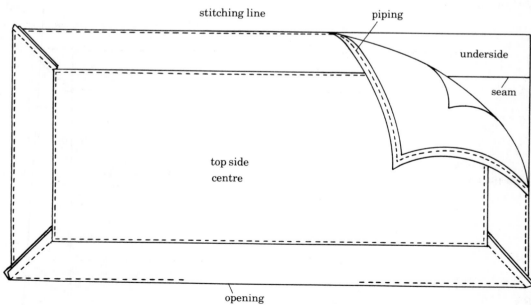

**386**

Place the eiderdown, top side uppermost, on the table. Place the completed cover on top with the inside facing the eiderdown. Sew the cover to each corner of the eiderdown using a strong thread. Lock stitch all round the outer edge of the cover securing it to the eiderdown. When the stitches have been completed, turn the cover, with the eiderdown attached, right side out **387.**

Push all the corners out to their fullest extent. Slipstitch the opening together. The eiderdown is now ready for the design to be pinned in. Using the tissue pattern pin to the eiderdown and follow the design **388.**

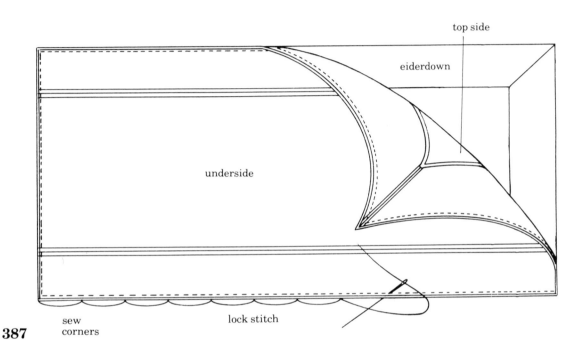

top side

eiderdown

underside

sew corners

lock stitch

**387**

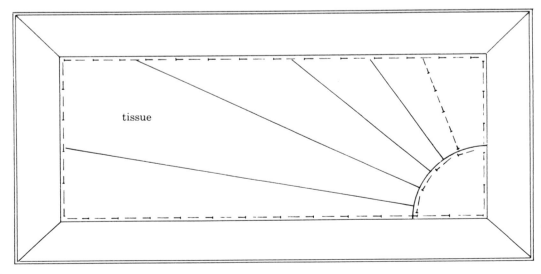

tissue

**388**

121

After pinning in the design, tack stitch the design through the tissue paper, remove the pins and then tear the paper away. Starting with the border, machine along the tacking lines. Hold the fabric taut when stitching, this will prevent the underside from tucking. Where the design is curved, try and stitch in a continual line, so as to get a clean curve. In a design with parallel lines, start and finish all the lines in the same direction, this prevents the fabric from twisting out of shape. Start and finish all ends securely, check that all the threads have been cut off. On a very full or puffy eiderdown, it is sometimes necessary to make provision for the air trapped between the bed and underside of the eiderdown. This is done by pushing a thick needle right through the eiderdown, at a point approximately 2 cm from the edge of the border (see diagrams) on all four corners. With a matching thread, buttonhole stitch all round the hole finishing neatly on the underside **389, 390.**

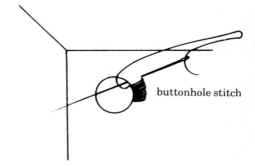

buttonhole stitch

**390** *Making an eyelet*

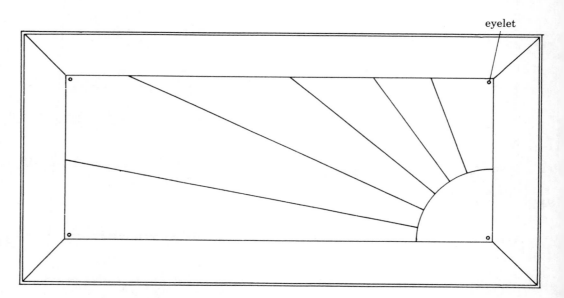

eyelet

**389** *Finished eiderdown with piped edge*

# 19: Patchwork

Although patchwork is not really classified as *Soft furnishing* (it would come under *Handicrafts*), it has grown in popularity and is now incorporated in soft furnishings, in bedcovers, cushions and duvet covers. Many books and articles have been written on the design and application of patchwork. I have therefore confined this chapter to the basic methods of making patchwork, both by hand and by machine. To make both types of patchwork, you must have an accurate template of the shapes to be used. These templates are available from handicraft shops, and can be metal or plastic **391.**

The metal templates are stronger, but the plastic templates have the advantage of being transparent which helps in centralising patterns if necessary. Select material of the same weight and thickness, cotton is ideal as it does not tend to fray. The colours need to blend to obtain a pleasing design. Using a sharp pencil, place the template on the fabric, and draw round it. For hand patchwork allow an extra $\frac{1}{2}$ cm all round for turnings. For machine patchwork cut to the pencil line as no turning is needed.

Cut a few dozen patches, in each colour, and place them in piles, this saves having to sort through to find the right colour. Cut paper templates for hand patchwork, to the exact size of the patch required.

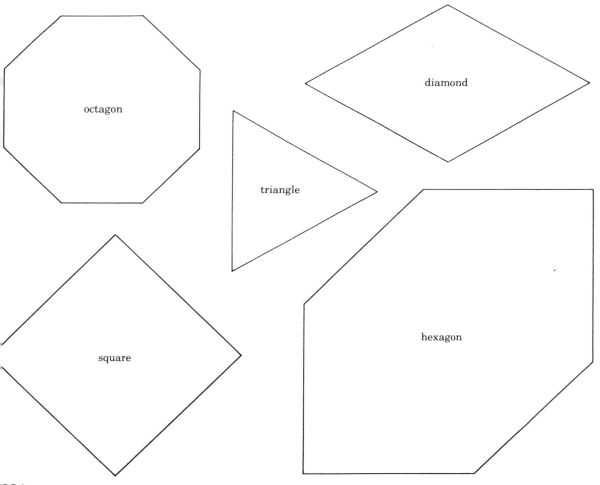

octagon

diamond

triangle

square

hexagon

**391** *A selection of shapes used in patchwork*

## Hand patchwork

After cutting the patches, both in fabric and paper, press the fabric and place it right side down. Place the paper patch on top and turn the fabric edges to cover the paper edges (see diagrams). Tack the fabric in place making sure the corners stay in place. Continue to cover paper patches until you have several piles of different colours **392, 393**.

Having made several piles of assorted patches, place them so that they make a pleasing design. Starting with the centre patch, sew the patches together by oversewing the edges **394**.

In the above design two patch shapes are used, but this is not always necessary. Almost every shape will repeat itself in a design without having a 'fill in' shape. Continue to stitch the patchwork shapes and when the whole design has been completed take out the paper templates. It is sometimes necessary to applique the patchwork to a firm fabric base (for example to use as a cushion) or to back the whole piece with interlining, and then turn in the edges and line it to make a bedcover.

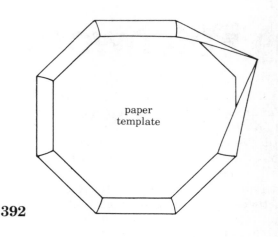

paper template

**392**

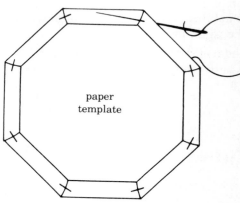

paper template

**393**

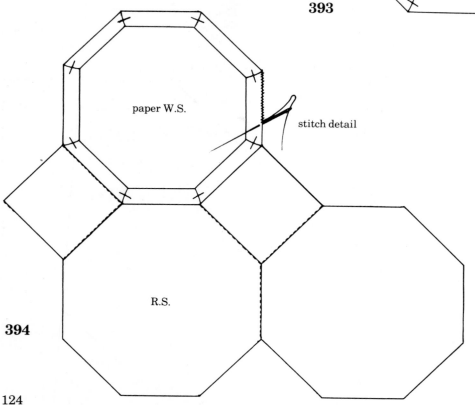

paper W.S.

stitch detail

R.S.

**394**

## Machine patchwork

Before machining the patches you will need iron-on Vilene. Cut the patches to the exact size of the template, and make sure they are accurate. Cut the piece of Vilene bigger than the finished article. Measure the Vilene both across and down and mark the exact centre, with pencil lines. To illustrate the process I have used the diamond shape as this will repeat itself indefinitely **395.**

*Effective use of machine patchwork on a cushion cover*

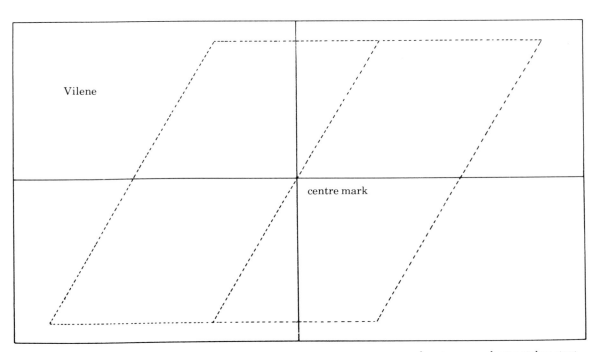

Vilene

centre mark

**395** *Marking the Vilene*

. . . denotes area where patches start

125

Pin the patches on to the Vilene, making sure the sticky side is uppermost on the Vilene. Press with a warm iron until the patches are firmly fused with the Vilene. Remove the pins, and thread the machine with a matching or blending embroidery thread. Using a zigzag stitch, machine along the joins, making sure that the edges are caught in. The closer the stitch the better, as it will make a definition between the patches, as well as making the seams strong.

When machining do not go round each individual patch, machine right across so that the stitching line remains unbroken. The patchwork is now ready to use in the making of a complete article **396.**

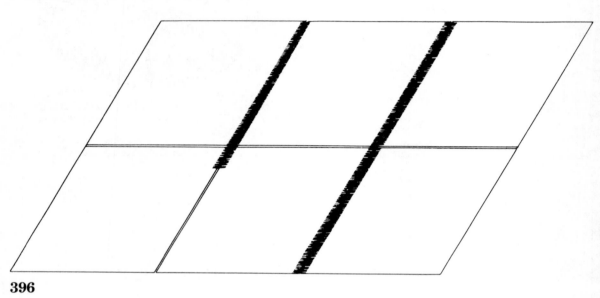

**396**

# Glossary

| | |
|---|---|
| *Cleat* | A way of tying the cords of a gathering tape to give a neat finish. |
| *Double skirt* | Two pieces of tape or fabric joined at the top edge, for example lining tape. |
| *Eye* | Part of the runner on a curtain rail; the curtain hook passes through the eye. |
| *Finials* | Decorative ends used on rods or poles as end stops. |
| *Notch* | A 'V' shape cut in the seam allowance; the notches are matched to ensure a perfect fit when assembling the article. |
| *Pelmet* | A cut-out shape in fabric or wood fitted in front of the rail mechanism to hide it. Can be decorative or plain. |
| *Soffit* | The plastered edge that is set immediately above the window frame. |
| *Square* | To square a piece of fabric means to cut it so that the edge is at right angles to the selvedge. |
| *Straight edge* | A length of wood or metal used to place on the fabric in order to draw a straight line. |
| *Tack tape* | Cotton webbing or tape sewn on to an article and then fixed in place with upholstery tacks. |
| *Tape back* | To bind the raw edges of the fabric with tape in order to neaten them. |
| *To the thread* | To cut between two threads usually following the line of the weft thread. |

# Index

# Useful addresses

**Association of Master Upholsterers**
  Dormar House, Mitre Bridge, Scrubs Lane, London NW10 6QB
  Tel: 01-965 3565

**Beckfoot Mill Ltd.** *(Fillings, materials)*
  Howden Road, Silsden, near Keighley, W. Yorks    Tel: 0535 53358

**Distinctive Trimmings Co. Ltd.** *(Gimps, braids, fringes, etc.)*
  17 Kensington Church Street, London W8 4LF    Tel: 01-937 6174
  *and* 11 Marylebone Lane W1.

**D. L. Forster Ltd.** *(Mail order only)*
  17 Tramway Avenue, Stratford, London E15 4PG

**ILEA London College of Furniture**
  41-71 Commercial Road, London E1 14A    Tel: 01-247 1953

**Louis Moreau (The Quilters) Ltd.**
  651 High Road, Tottenham, London N17 8AA    Tel: 01-808 1337

*Manufacturers of curtain products (Track, poles, tapes etc.)*

**Antiference Ltd.** *(Kirsch, Decorail, etc.)*
  Bicester Road, Aylesbury, Bucks HP19 3BJ    Tel: 0296-82511

**Harrison-Beacon Ltd.** *(Drape, Supertracks, etc.)*
  Bradford Street, Birmingham B12 0PE    Tel: 021-773 1111

**Rufflette Ltd.**
  Sharston Road, Wynthenshawe, Manchester M22 4TH
  Tel: 061-998 1811
  *or* 59 St. James Street, London SW1    Tel: 01-629 7101

**Swish Products Ltd.**
  Beechfield Road Industrial Estate, Tamworth, Staffordshire
  B79 7TW    Tel: 0827-3811

*Local libraries will have lists or prospectuses of adult education classes.*